WRITERS!
START YOUR MEMOIRS!

Tips and Techniques:

What,

Then What,

So What

Kathy Tuten, BA MEd

So why write a memoir in the first place?

Because you have a story to tell!

Because only you can tell your story!

Only you can find the extraordinary in the ordinary of your own life. And that is worth telling.

You have a set of life experiences that only you have had and only you can share.

You have at least one amazing story to tell that you have never even thought about putting on paper until now.

If you don't tell your story we may lose historical perspectives that absolutely should be passed along to future generations. After all, think about all the stories we have already lost!

You want to ensure that your children and grandchildren know their family history through you.

You want to write about your most significant relationship(s).

You want to get even with someone, or the world, for that matter, by setting the record straight.

You have overcome a great obstacle, physical or mental, and you think that sharing the story of how you got through it might help others in the same situation.

You want to settle a score! Yes, you know who you want to call out……

You want to be a writer. You've thought about writing for a long time and never quite knew where to start. And finally you've thought about a good starting place: your own fascinating life.

You just feel a need to get your life down on paper.

About This Book:

If you've had thoughts about setting your life down on paper, here's a place to start!

Everyone has a story to tell but not everyone has any idea how to start telling it. And not knowing how to start out keeps many would-be memoirists from setting down a really good story.

In the writing classes I teach I frequently ask my students: if you don't tell your story, who will? And I am eternally grateful to those who have gone before for keeping journals, writing letters, taking photographs, and making films. Otherwise we might never know about significant historic events, both good and evil. Or we would only have the sanitized versions to be found in textbooks. Or we might only have the fictionalized versions we see in the movies. We might never know how events shaped ordinary folks or how ordinary folks shaped historical events.

So, even if you're an 'ordinary folk' you do have a story to tell.

I first started thinking about memoirs, on a much smaller scale, several years ago when my youngest sibling died quite suddenly and unexpectedly leaving a wife and two small children. It occurred to me that his children would never know what their legacy was from their father if somebody didn't put something down on paper to tell them what a great kid he was and how he fit into our family and why they turned out the way *they* did (!). So I put together a memoir through pictures and artifacts of my brother's life for his children. And added a narrative to it. And that one was so successful I did one for each of my other siblings.

Then, since I write handbooks on various topics, I thought I ought to share what I've learned along the way. So this handbook is designed to help you tell your own story. It's a *very* practical handbook. It's got:

- 40+ Workspaces to help you unlock your memories and get some ideas onto paper. I love to include actual space in my handbooks for people to write in so no one has to go digging for paper, and all kinds of notes and lists can be kept all in the same place! And there's no particular order to the Workspaces: you can just do them in any order you like, or skip some of them altogether.
- Guidance on how to organize your manuscript
- Tips on how to outline your manuscript
- Tips on how to interview people in your life that you want to include in your memoir
- Guidance on what to put in and what to leave out
- Help with finding places to do your research
- Descriptions of several kinds of memoirs that might appeal to the writer in you
- Advice on how to deal with the bad stuff as well as the good stuff
- Help with deciding if your memoir is just for your family or if it really needs to be published
- Tips on how to hold your story together so it reads like a fiction best-seller!

It *doesn't* have:

- Lots of philosophizing
- Grammar and sentence structure exercises
- How to write dialogue
- How to get published, or self-publish
- Advice on writers' groups
- How to find an agent
- How to find an editor
- How to get your book into bookstores

Those are the kinds of things you can find in a writing textbook.

This is your basic toolkit for figuring out what you want to say.

And how to 'recover' memories.

And how you want to say it.

And where to go to find out what you don't know and can't at first figure out where to find.

And how to put it all together.

And how to write it like a novel best seller.

So start anywhere you want to in the handbook and go for it!

Section 1:

Some General Information

Memoir Workspace 1: What Do You Think You Want to Say?

You want to write your memoir. There are many ways to start out and many ways to organize your memoir but you first have to think about what you want to say. What is the most important thing you want us, the readers, to know about you?

1. Write your memoir in only 6 words – yes, I said 6 words!

   Why did you choose those particular words?

2. Write down in one paragraph of no more than 10 sentences what you think your memoir will be about:

3. Make a list of a dozen 'firsts' you can remember from your life: the first birthday party you can remember, your first day of school, your first love:

   -
   -
   -
   -
   -
   -
   -
   -

-
-
-
-

4. Now, you might have to think about this one: what's the major story of your life that you tell yourself? What is the major theme of your life as you see it? When you talk to yourself in your own head what kinds of things are you most likely saying to yourself about yourself?

Memoir: The Basics

What makes a memoir a memoir and not an autobiography?

First, a memoir depends more on your *memories* of things that really happened in your past than an autobiography does. In an autobiography, you stick much more to concrete events and the times and dates and places you've been. So, for example, I started school on this date, and I graduated from high school on this date and on this date and time I attended this specific writing conference, and so on and so on. An autobiography covers much more territory of your life than a memoir might. An autobiography is basically a straight history of your life, with research on facts, dates, specific places, and your 'place' in the history of your life as you fit into the broader history of the world (yes, world!).

In a memoir you go back through your memories and write them down. A memoir is how you remember your life, which may be very different from how everyone around you remembers you. Very simple, right? Welllll. Maybe not so much. You need to put some time into thinking things through so you get the memories down in a structure that you like.

What makes a memoir a memoir and not a novel?

In a novel you can let your story-telling flow free and literally make it up as you go along. In a memoir you need to stick pretty much to the truth, although your memories are *your* memories and not anyone else's. You may remember things differently from other people who were in the same room with you at the same time an incident occurred. That's perfectly fine. Just be sure you are telling the best truth you can tell as you remember it.

In a novel, we readers can usually see all the internal workings of most, if not all, of the characters. We can see what they are thinking and how they are feeling all the way through the story. In a memoir, you have to stick to how *you* are thinking and feeling. Although you may be able to get strong feelings from someone else, or you may intuit how they are feeling, you need to make sure you're sticking to *your* feelings and thoughts most of the time.

Easy enough, right? Well, again, maybe not so much...... The problem with memoirs is that sometimes you remember something entirely different from the way it really happened. That can cause a problem when a memory blurs with the actual truth. What if what you remember doesn't really jibe with what really happened? So you might have to tread lightly in some places, but remember: these are *your* memories.

How are memoirs and autobiographies and novels alike?

They all three tell a story. They all three have a beginning, a middle, and an end. Depending on the form of the writing, the story is about a fictional character, or a real person, you and your life by the numbers, or your best memories of your life as you have lived it. If you haven't got a story, you haven't got a novel or an autobiography or a memoir.

But the best part all the way around is that everyone has a story..........

Memoir Workspace 2: Unlocking Memories

Unlocking your memories can be difficult. Here's an exercise that might help.

Draw a self-portrait of you at 5 or 7 or 12 with your favorite colors. It doesn't make any difference if all you've got is a stick figure. Use colored pencils, crayons, markers, whatever you have around. Then think about what your choice of colors says about you and your memories.

Now draw a self-portrait of you as you are today. What's the biggest difference you see?

So what are the basic rules for writing a memoir?

1. It needs to be about the length of any other published book, fiction or nonfiction. That means between about 60,000 and 120,000 words. Don't worry. You might start with only a few pages, maybe only one memory that you write about. But once you let the writer in you loose, the words will come, and then the pages will come.

2. You don't need to tell every detail of every memory in your life. Your memoir will be far more interesting if you focus on a certain number of memories: limit the number of memories you write about to the ones you yourself find most interesting as you think about them. No one actually needs to know what you feed your dog…..

3. Be honest, as far as you can remember. Tell the truth as you know/knew it. Your memories are your memories and your 'truth' about an episode in your life may be very different from anyone else's memory of the same incident. But stick as close as you can to what you know or knew to be true at the time.

4. Tell 'mini-stories' as you work through your memories. All good narratives, whether fiction or nonfiction, have a beginning, a middle, and an end. Each of your memories and their connections to one another will be more effective if you follow that same path.

5. Use colorful language, use specific descriptions of events and people. The more descriptive you can be about a situation or a character in your memoir the more interesting your readers will find you. In this instance adjectives and adverbs are your friends. You probably cannot over-describe your characters.

6. If one, or more, of your characters faces a conflict of their own, tell it as honestly as you can, especially if their conflict impacts your own life directly. It's important in your own life story to tell how you worked through your relationship with this particular person.

7. Use dialogue sparingly and mostly only when you were actually present to hear the words spoken out loud. Trying to remember a conversation from 30 years ago verbatim is not going to help you with your own truths. It's best just to paraphrase and then react in your own way to a conversation on your own pages.

8. Research what you don't remember or aren't sure about. Think about letters, cards, notes, diaries, archives. Do your research as much as possible before you even start writing. It will help you get over any page fright you might have when you sit down in front of a blank piece of paper.

Memoir Skeleton

Unlike fiction and autobiography, memoirs can be more flexible as far as 'plot' and/or chronology go. However, there are some things you need to remember as you begin a memoir. Like fiction especially, if you remember these ribs of a memoir skeleton, you will find writing your memoir much easier. Just as in a human skeleton, you can't take out – leave out – too many ribs or the whole thing will collapse.

1. A memoir focuses on only specific parts of your life, those parts that are most meaningful to you, unlike an autobiography, which tries to capture every event in life from birth to death.

2. You must be truthful as much as you can be with your memories.

3. Tell your story as you remember it – a real narrative.

4. As in a fictional narrative, your 'story' will resonate with readers if you describe your characters fully.

5. As in a fictional narrative, some drama in the process of telling your story helps. If there's no drama, people won't keep on reading.

6. Your memoir does NOT have to be chronological.

7. One purpose your memoir serves is to help give some kind of meaning to your life's events, helping to organize your thoughts and feelings about your past experiences.

8. A memoir uncovers and confronts the truths about what has happened to you during your life.

9. A memoir helps you discover who you really are.

10. A memoir preserves some of your family's most important history.

11. In a memoir you may absolutely *exclude* parts of your life you don't want to write about.

12. As in fiction, narrative conflicts in a memoir keep people reading. So you might want to explore some of those conflicts you 've faced in your life, big or small.

13. Memoirs follow one of the following set patterns:
    a. Flashback: depicting entire scenes of your past as you remember them, maybe not in chronological order but in an order that is important to you.
    b. Exposition: you let someone else, one of your characters, do the work of revealing your history through straight narrative
    c. Detail: you focus on the details of incidents to move your story forward; in other words, minute description, maybe focusing most on sounds, or sights, or smells, or touches (textures

14. Memoirs follow one of the following four structures:
    a. Chronological
    b. Semi-autobiographical
    c. Episodic
    d. Thematic

15. The writer of a memoir is the star of the memoir, not a supporting player. So the major focus, the plot if you will, always stays with the star. The focus needs to stay on the memoirist and what happens around him/her, and shouldn't wander off into the life stories of peripheral players.

How do you set up a memoir?

So, let's think about those four structures. What do they mean? How do you do each one?

The chronological memoir may seem like the easiest way for you to get those important events of your life down on paper. You're telling your life's story from the beginning, or close to the beginning. This is probably the most popular structure for memoirs. You pick a specific point to start your story, you describe that instance, and then you go from the next instance to the next instance to the next instance pretty much in the order the instances happened to you. The element of time is built into this form of memoir. There's a first, a second, a third, and so on. What makes this format easy to follow and write down is that it's sequential. It's logical. It's linear, in other words. However, understand that you can't really explain point 12 until you've finished with point 10. But you have to…..

In a chronological memoir, however, you don't necessarily have to start with your birth. You can start at any point that's important to you, even if your first important memory occurs at age 10 or 12. So, you can describe events when you were 10, when you were 14, when you were 18, when you were 25. But be careful: you can't skip around. You can't do age 12, and then 14, and then 24 and then 18 and then 44. You still need to follow the logical sequence of your years, in this instance.

You don't even have to include everything that happens to you in each of those years just because one or two interesting things happened in one year. Skip the years that, to you, were kind of ordinary. Nothing in particular happened that stood out to you. Readers like to see the logical sequence of events, but they don't really mind if you skip over the dinners at home with family, or the movies you loved, or the time your best friend dunked you in the pond. They want to hear about the important stuff!

Chronological order is the simplest of the memoir forms.

The semiautobiographical memoir is a more fragmented format than the chronological memoir. In this format you may tell your story in some chronological sections, so you may go from one year to the next for several important events. But then you may take a 'break' from the recalling of events and talk to your readers about what else was going on in the world during a particular sequence of events. Or you may 'philosophize' about how you felt yourself fitting into the world around you at the time. Or you may just think on paper about the events you've described. Think about *Sex and the City,* in which Carrie, the main character, periodically speaks directly to the viewing audience to explain the inner workings of what's going on with the characters.

You can still organize this format easily if you just 'chunk' your recollections. So, write out three events and then a break, three events and then a 'conversation' break, three events and then a break. Remember that you are writing what's important to you, so your thoughts about life as a whole are important to the 'plot' of your memoir.

You can also arrange this format by scenes/settings, or maybe by characters in your life. You still tell them in chronological order as each setting becomes important to you, or a new important person enters your life. But you can leave out the unimportant (to you) bits about the places you've been and other people you've known.

The semi-autobiographical order is most like many popular TV sitcoms, which skip from scene to scene or person to person but still keep the story moving forward during their 30 or 60 minute time slots. So you know this format will work with many readers.

The episodic memoir may be a little harder to wrestle with, but it can be a very powerful format. In this format you have decided on the 10 or 15 or 20 most important events that have ever happened to you in your life. Or even the *one* event that changed your life. Then you describe each event thoroughly and completely from its beginning to its end. This format requires perhaps more thinking through before you write so you can get to the truly important stuff. So you don't necessarily have to retell events as they happened in time. You could describe them in order of import to you: most to 'least;' most painful to least painful; most traumatic to least traumatic; funniest to 'least' funny. In other words, you're going to write about your life's few most impactful incidents or occasions, and skip all the other stuff.

In the episodic structure you would be wise to give each of your events its own chapter, or its own section of a chapter. Each chapter will look on its pages kind of like a one hour television program: it has its own beginning, middle, and end. And then you can move on to the next separate instance. This format adds interest to readers by keeping things short and self-contained. So a reader could pick up your memoir and start at the middle rather than at the beginning, if that's what interests them.

You still want to have some kind of overarching plan to your memoir even if you like this format best. You need a some kind of broad theme to write around, or a place to write around or a person to write around. What makes this format work really well is if you show readers that there is a structure to your plan. You can easily divide your chapters and sometimes you can use a 'cliffhanger' at the end of one chapter to spur your readers to keep going into the next chapter.

The best thing about episodic memoirs is that you just simply start each chapter with the beginning of an event and write through to the end of that event. Then, on to the next chapter. So there's no worry about where or when to break up your information. Think about *Tuesdays with Maury,* which is divided into 'chapters' that describe each of the author's sit-down meetings with his mentor, and talk about the lessons he learned from Maury, who was dying and had had a full life.

The thematic memoir is written around one theme or, at the most, two themes. This is a little more difficult to do and requires some advance planning to make sure you can carry through with your theme from beginning of memoir to end. In this case you don't think necessarily about time frames or 'plots' or logical sequences. You choose a theme that is important to you and your memoir revolves around that theme.

So, for example, your theme is your mother's death from cancer and all that taught you. Or, the great love of your life lost and rediscovered. Or, your child's fight with a life threatening disease and what that taught you. Or it could be less emotionally charged: your life as an ambassador's kid and all the places you lived and what each one taught you. But whatever theme you pick, you have to stick to that theme. You can't go off sideways into your high school experience or how much you love the ocean or how successful your children are, if they aren't part of your overall theme.

So, in the beginning of your memoir you introduce the theme. You develop the theme through your memories and your descriptions of events around that theme, what you learned, what you wish you had learned, what you know now that you didn't know then. You do need to get to a logical end point at the end of this type of memoir. You do need to pull all those thematic threads together for your readers. But you need to go deeper than just bringing your readers up to date on your life in general. You need to have explored your theme for the benefit of your readers, as well as for your own benefit.

The thematic memoir focuses much more on events and things and happenings than it does on characters, so this might be more to your liking if you find people difficult to describe. Or if you have had what you think are some really important or trying or fabulously successful events in your life. Just remember that we human beings just love closure in our literature as we do in our lives, so come full circle, back to the beginning, as you finish the thematic format.

Thematic memoirs have become very popular, in part because they not only focus on one particular part of a person's life, but they frequently offer readers pertinent insights into how the memoir writer survived a difficult situation. And what lessons the writer learned. And how the reader might profit from those life lessons.

A good example here is *Beautiful Boy: A Father's Journey Through His Son's Addiction* by David Sheff; you can tell the theme simply by reading the title.

Memoir Workspace 3: Your Block

Sketch out the block you grew up on. Or, if you moved more than once as a child, sketch your favorite block. Make sure you include plants and people and pets, and anything else you can remember.

Now write down a story you can remember from that block and that time in your life. You can focus on yourself or someone else or a pet or something about the block itself that you remember.

Memoir Workspace 4: Old Photos

Go find some old photos that have you in them. Or find an old scrapbook or an old box of photos. Look through the photos and jot down the following:

1. What kinds of facial expressions do you see –of yourself - in most photos? Pick one photo that really speaks to you about something you remember from your younger days. If you had to tell us how you were feeling in this photo in only one or two words, how would you describe yourself? Cheerful? Happy? Worried? Sad? Bored? Why do you choose that word?

2. Now write a good paragraph about what's going on in the photo to the best of your knowledge. What do you remember?

Memoir Workspace 5: Basic Research

This is an exercise you can easily do nowadays, especially with the Internet.
Start with the year you were born and find the following information:

1. Find the *New York Times* bestseller list for that year. List two or three titles from the fiction list:

   •

   •

   •

2. List two or three titles from the nonfiction list:

   •

   •

   •

3. What do these titles tell you about what people were thinking about that year?

4. Find the *Time Magazine* Person of the Year. (You might not be old enough to remember, but it used to be called "Time's Man of the Year"). What does the selection of this person tell you about what people were thinking at that time?

5. Find your hometown newspaper. Scroll through or flip through some of the pages.

•   What kinds of advertisements are there?

•   What are some of the headlines?

•   What are some of the comics?

•   What do these pieces of information tell you about what was going on at that time? About what people valued – or not – at that time?

6. Get on the internet and on Wikipedia. Look up the year you were born. What does Wikipedia list that was going on in that year? You aren't going to remember any of those things, but when you get into your memoir this information may very well help you with your parents, your grandparents, your other older relatives, and you will be able to plug in what they were thinking and how they felt.

-

-

-

-

-

-

7. Find an almanac from the year you were born. You can use a print one but they are also easy to find on the internet.   What was going on in:

- medicine

- government

- religion

- theater and movies

- sports

- science

- the economy

8. What does this almanac information tell you about the times you were born into?

9. How do you think these things intersected with who you have become? Or did they influence your life at all?

Memoir Workspace 6: Scrapbooks and Yearbooks

1. Find an old scrapbook, either one of your own, or if you don't have one, one someone close to you has. What's in it of interest?

   a.

   b.

   c.

   d.

   e.

   f.

   g.

2. Why do these particular items strike you as interesting? What do they say to you about you?

3. Find a high school or college yearbook. Or even an elementary school one if you have one. What's in it that's interesting?

      a.

      b.

      c.

      d.

      e.

4. Why do these particular pieces of information strike you as interesting? What do they say about you to you?

5. Did you find any items or pieces of information *missing* from either book? Somebody's picture cut out, for example? What do omissions say to you about you?

Now for the organization piece.

Now that you've got some basic research done, regardless of which of the four basic types of memoir you think you might like to write, it's time to think about making an outline. Many people in this world are good, even great, writers, who seemingly write like they are possessed by the Genie of Great Writing: the words just magically appear and arrange themselves on the page! But, trust me; the largest majority of those writers have some kind of an outline in their minds when they set out to write the first pages. Some writers can keep all their plot lines and characters and scenes in their heads, but most put something down on paper to remember where they started, where they want to go, and how they want to end. You would probably be smart to make some kind of plan before you start your writing.

The simplest of outlines is:

1. Start with a title. I know, I know, you don't have a title yet. But put something down on paper for a title. You'll be surprised how much that spurs you on.
2. Decide what's the most important point you want to get across to everyone else about your life. That's the point that will grab your readers' interest and keep them wanting to read on. (That's going to become your first chapter. Remember: you want to 'hook' your readers quickly.)
3. Decide on the second most important point or event in your life. That may be Chapter 2.
4. The third point. That may be Chapter 3.
5. And so on.
6. From all these points together you can make a 'map' of your memories and how you want to tell them.

So, you've got a built-easy outline.

An outline, even if you cringe at the thought of writing one out, is important for several reasons.

1. You don't get yourself confused by your 'plot.' If you get confused, and you're the one doing the writing, just imagine how confused your readers will get! And that's *not* something you want to happen.
2. You don't get bogged down as you write. You don't get lost and meander around, and perhaps include too much extraneous information, or leave out something really important.
3. You don't write and write and write and then discover after 152 pages that you're not saying what you want to say. You're going around in large circles. You've lost your thread of thought. And you've wasted a lot of time and effort (and brains!) on writing something that's just not good.
4. You can refer to your outline any time as you go along to make sure you're still on track to write what you think is important. In other words, an outline can help you focus on the 'big picture' and not on all the little life-sapping details. It can help you remember why your story is so important to tell, and keep you from writing about all that stuff that in retrospect wasn't so important after all.

Some other kinds of outlines that might appeal to your sense of organization:

Flowchart outline: this is your basic old-timey outline. It starts with your thesis statement at the top. So:

I.   Small town detective must solve the vicious murder of an old lady

A. Old lady is found murdered and we need to find out who did it

1. It turns out that many people in small town didn't like her and could have murdered her, so who did it?

a. People who could have had a grudge

1. list names of people

b. people who were around her home at the time

1. list names of people

II.   Suspects interviewed
A.   First suspect
1.   first interview
2.   second interview
B.   Second suspect
1.   First interview
2.   Second interview

And on down...

V. Closing in

A. "Persons of interest" after interviews

1.   Person 1
2.   Person 2

And so on. Basically you think through your memories as you've dug them up so far and put them in some kind of order. This type of outline works best if you're going to write a chronological memoir. One good thing about this outline is that you can get as specific on paper as you want to or you can just go for the bigger ideas at first and fill in the little letters later.

If you're a linear-sequential thinker (and you know who you are!) this is the outline for you!

Note card outline: this is an outline format in which you write a significant memory on the top of a big note card (use 5 x 8s, don't use the little dinky ones) and then write what you think of immediately as you can. Write down what specific things you remember about that scene. Don't worry if your thoughts aren't in order. When you've done as many notecards as you have memories, what you can do to get to some kind of order is line them all up on the kitchen table, or on your desk, just randomly, or you could even stick them up on a blank wall. Walk yourself through them and rearrange them, and rearrange them, and rearrange them. Eventually, you'll find an order that makes sense to you, and you're on your way.

For some people, the act of physically moving the cards around helps to solidify the order that makes the most sense to them. So go for an order that you like, and then maybe number the cards so you remember your order, and start writing.

Be aware that you might end up not using each and every notecard. Just set aside the ones you think you don't need for the moment. As you get into your draft memoir you might find some cards that you can't fit in. When you get all your cards done look for the ones that reflect your major theme or your major episodes. Don't think that you must use every card. One of the best things about this outline method is that you can pull out what isn't working at the moment and save those cards for your second memoir! This outline works well if you're going for the episodic or the thematic memoir.

It may end up looking something like this:

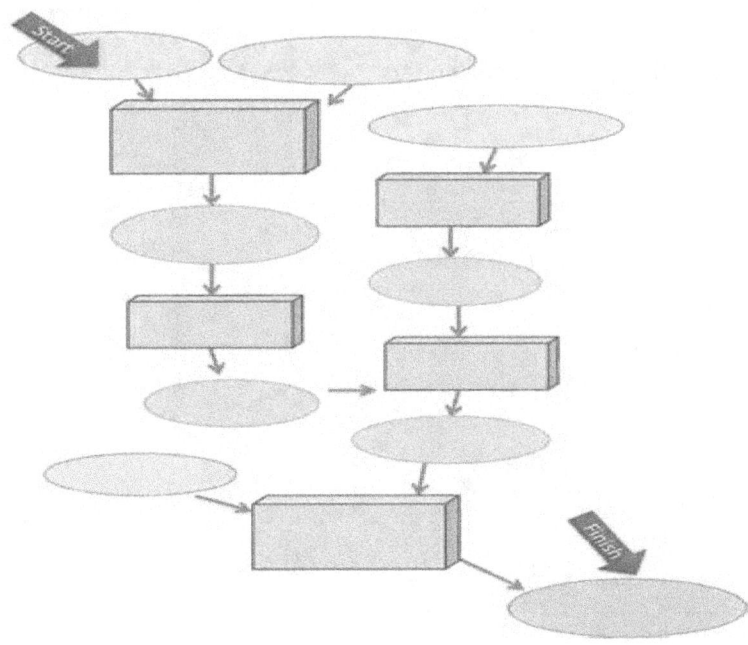

<u>Montage outline</u>: this type of outline looks like those white boards you see on the new mystery/cop shows on TV (*Castle* comes to mind here). You can literally take a space in your house or office and stick your 'memories' onto it. You can put up photos and old dance notices, souvenir programs from your favorite concerts, and old love letters, note cards and sticky notes, programs and church bulletins. These are your life's 'artifacts'. Whatever you have that's important to you. Put everything up as you come to it. Then you have a couple of options. Move things around on your 'board' till the order begins to make sense to you. Or, if you're the artsy/craftsy type, put your artifacts on a sheet of poster paper, or several sheets if you need them, get a couple of old balls of yarn and connect the dots from artifact to artifact with some push pins, and going in an order you like. You could color code the artifacts with different yarns. Use some kind of marker to place the artifacts in the order you like, maybe number them or use a lettering system.

The good thing about this type of outline is that if you're a visually-oriented person the physical artifacts will speak to you may be better than the written words on the flowchart outline. You can certainly use photos of your artifacts instead of the artifacts themselves. This outline works really well for the thematic or episodic memoir, although you can certainly use it for the chronological memoir as well. Again, though, don't think you must use every artifact on your board. You might find some things just don't fit so save them for your next book.

It may end up looking something like this:

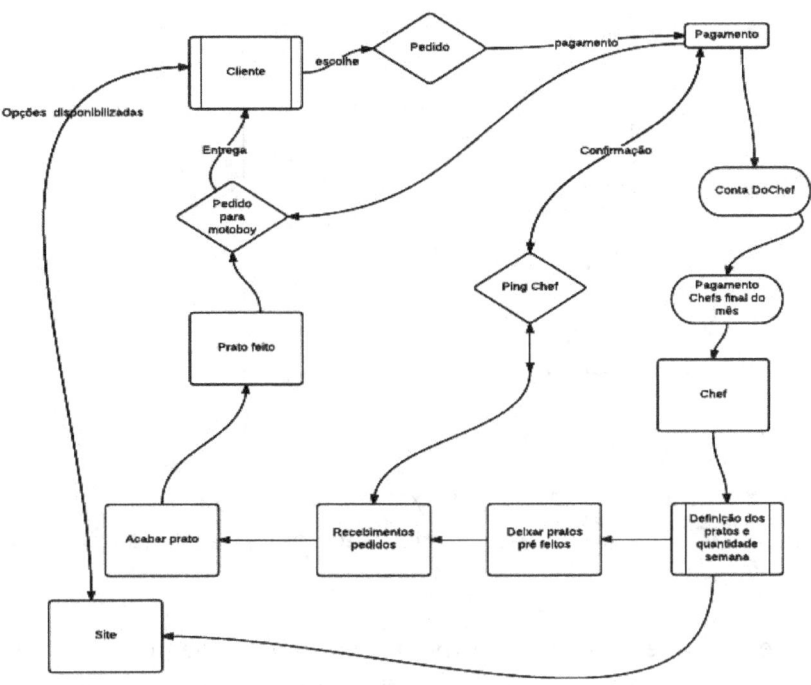

Mind map outline: this type of outline is useful if you're looking for connections among your memories or if you have the 'big picture' memory and you want to delve deeper into it to make it more meaningful for yourself. This type of outline may not be familiar to lots of adults but (just so you know) teachers use it with great success when trying to get across important ideas to students. Again, get some note cards and maybe a big sheet of paper or a blank wall.   Put your main memory (theme) in the center block. For each thought you have about your memory, put that in one of the boxes around the center. By the time you're through with this memory, you may have a whole section of writing drafted. And actually, you can take the mind map another step farther by going out into more blocks as your secondary thoughts bring more thoughts to mind.

Add blocks as far as you want to go, but when you start the actual writing don't feel like you have to use all of the blocks. Some may end up not fitting your purpose. If you put a blank mind map on its own sheet of paper you could do one for each of your memories, or each of the important people in your memoir, or each important setting, and so on.

This type of outline is very useful to the episodic and the thematic memoir, although if you're going for a chronological memoir, you can use a mind map to put your memories in order; just get them down first and then rearrange the sheets of paper in chronological order. Don't forget to number the sheets (in case you should drop the whole stack!).

It may look something like this:

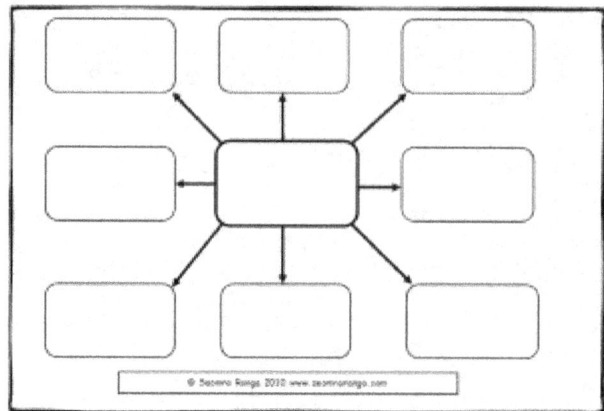

The important thing is to use some kind of outline, just to keep yourself organized. Use any of the outline formats above, make up one of your own, or use a combination of two or more of the outlines as you think through what you want to write.

You may also find a 'mini-outline' useful as you get into the middle of your memoir. You might find there's a section you're having a hard time with. It's not going right, or you're not sure how to move it forward past a certain point. Or it might not seem as if it's in the right place in the grand scheme of things.

If you find yourself going around in circles about one segment of your memoir, drop back and think a bit. Then outline how you would like *just that section* to go. Use any of the outlines you find here or just do a bulleted list of incidences and incidents and issues that you want to be sure to put into that section. Then, rewrite the section according to your new mini-outline. Even if your mini-outline just goes in chronological order, that gives you a springboard to start from.

And there are no "outline police" as far as I know. So if you think of things as you go along, nothing stops you from revising your outline. After you get some kind of outline done, add to it, subtract from it, move parts of it around to suit your "plot." You're still keeping yourself organized!

Now, one caveat: if you get bogged down in following your outline and you feel your memoir is not going in the right direction, not going where you want it, *do not be afraid to dump part of your outline!* Go back in your manuscript to where you *were* happy with it. Redo your outline from that point on. There's no need to reinvent the whole thing; just backtrack to where you were on a good roll and reconceptualize your 'plot' from that point forward. You absolutely need to give yourself permission to redo if you're totally bogged down.....

Second caveat: if you *do* decide to redo your outline *don't throw away the old one.* You may eventually find that some parts of it come in handy as you revise the new outline. Or you may pull some parts of it for a whole new memoir

Memoir Workspace 8: Early Person You Admired

- Who was the person you most admired when you were growing up? Why did you admire this person so much?

- What did this person teach you that has stuck with you?

bbr

Memoir Workspace 9: It Used to Matter but...

1. The 5 things that seemed to matter to me the most when I was in high school/college were:
    *

    *

    *

    *

    *

2. The 5 things that matter most to me now are:
    *

    *

    *

    *

    *

3. What do the similarities/differences between these two lists tell you about yourself?

Memoir Workspace 10: Books

1. The book I've read that has influenced me most in my life was/is:

2. I liked the book because:

3. The most important thing that book taught me was:

Other places to find information:

So what kinds of pieces of information can you use to cull your memories from?

Are you a blogger?

Do you keep old scrapbooks?

Do you keep a journal?

Do you keep a diary?

Do you keep photo albums?

Do you keep letters or cards or notes?

Do you keep bulleted lists of your important occasions, or 'things to do'?

❖ Those are all good sources of information about your life.

If you're not a journaler or diarist, you might buy one of those little hardback books you can get at any big box store and write a few words or sentences on each page every day. Those little books frequently give writing prompts on many pages, and you can get some good information on yourself by just jotting a few notes, even if you find you can't do it every day. Once you've got a few pages down, you can begin to pull from them what you want to tell about yourself.

Even if what you write in a journal or diary is painful to read over after you've written it, your pain or sorrow or anger or confusion is still a critical part of your writing journey, so don't ignore the bad parts. For you to gain some insight into yourself you need all those reflections on how you feel to make your portrait in writing complete.

If you're a blogger, especially if you're a long time blogger, you are most likely to blog about one or two subjects that are important to you, and probably important to other people too. Your blog might lead you to a thematic memoir. You have some important things to say to people about at least one subject, so go back and pull what you think are your best blogs, see if they do indeed focus on one major theme, and structure your memoir around that theme. If you want to write a memoir but you're not sure how to structure it, use your blogs!

Old scrapbooks are also windows into you and your life. What kinds of artifacts have you saved? Why? They must have some relevance to your life as you have lived it. Why have you kept those artifacts and not some others? Is there some kind of pattern to the things you've saved in your scrapbooks? Even if most of your scrapbooks are about your children or grandchildren, what you've kept in them still says reams about you. How you feel about being a mother or father. How you reacted to your first grandchild. How your much adored pet impacted your life. How your life revolved for several years around your wins in soccer, or dance contests, or art contests, or your winning football season. Go back and look through those old books to see what you remember. You can come back to it later and flesh out those memories in the right place.

Make a scrapbook right now of the 'artifacts' you *can* find: pictures, photos, letters, cards, notes, souvenirs, whatever pieces of paper you can find that have been important to you in the past. Again, don't worry about structure; just make a note on each one to remind you of its significance. Sticky notes are a good way to start keeping track of your 'stuff.'

Round up physical artifacts if you can. That means photos in frames on the wall. Coffee mugs. Beer mugs. Hats. Tee-shirts. Bracelet charms. Jewelry. Programs. Maps. Schedules. Whatever you have as a remembrance of a person, place, or thing. Put a sticky not on or under or in each one to remind you later why you saved it in the first place.

If you have travelled somewhere interesting in the past, and kept a journal or notes to go with what you experienced, pull that out now too.

Bankers boxes that you can buy at office supply stores are great for just chucking things into until you have the time and energy to get them organized.

The point to this section is to make sure you understand that you have multiple resources, and maybe many of them, to use as you start to think about a memoir. Don't think you have nothing to start with. Just look at all the possibilities you already have available to you. Make use of them. Go dig them out. Search the attic or the closets or the book shelves or the storage locker. Round up what you have right at your fingertips, even before you begin researching big time, and get started with what you have.

Memoir Workspace 11: Talents

1. When I was young I was really good at:

    •

    •

    •

    •

2. Now I'm really good at:

    •

    •

    •

    •

3. What's the most significant difference between the two lists?

Memoir Workspace 12: Death

1. The first time I encountered someone who had died was:

2. What was your relationship with that person?

3. What did you take away from that experience?

4. What have you learned about yourself as a result of that experience?

Memoir Workspace 13: Best Friends

1. The three best friends I've ever had are/were:

-
-
-

2. What made each one of them special to you?

-
-
-

3. Are they still your friends? If so, why? If not, why not?

-
-
-

4. What have your friends taught you about yourself?

Start with Mom and Pop.

Here's a starting point – at any point, really – that will help you go *way* back in time, your time that is. Buy your mother or your father a good cup of coffee or tea or a glass of wine or a beer and ask them to help you with your earliest days. These interview questions are good to use with other relatives: your grandmother, your grandfather, your aunt or uncle, your parents' long-time next door neighbor.

Some questions to get you started with this interview:

- How is the world different today from what it was when I was born?
- What did the family enjoy doing together before I was born and when I was a baby?
- What's your first memory of me?
- What's the funniest thing I ever did when I was little?
- What's the strangest thing I ever did when I was little?
- What do you think is the most important decision I've ever made in my life?
- If you were to describe me to someone who's never met me, never seen me, how would you describe me?
- What do you think is the biggest mistake I ever made in my life? Why do you think this was my worst one?
- What's something, or several things, that happened to me or that I did when I was little, or younger, that you think I should include in my memoir? Why?

If you have some longtime friends, ask them these same questions, and you might also want to ask:

- What's the biggest trouble we ever got into when we were kids?
- What's the best time we ever had when we were kids?

When you get your notes together you can use one of the outline forms described above to get them organized. You can also literally lay the answers to the questions side by side by side and see how other people knew you when you were growing up. What might be very interesting or revealing to you is if you find that different friends or relatives have some ideas or memories of you that are very different from one another, and maybe even very different from how you remember them. That's OK. Those differences will probably make for a very interesting memoir!

However, be sure you ask the same core of questions to each person you interview. You want to make sure you *can* compare notes. Make sure you keep the same 6 or 8 or 10 questions over all interviews. Then you can diverge if the interview goes in some other direction. It may turn out to be fascinating what you learn from someone who suddenly remembers something about you that you hadn't even thought about. But at least you've got several perspectives on the same information to start from.

Some general interview tips:

When you find someone who has interesting and/or important things to say about you and the people you're writing about, think about the following:

1. Never ask questions that can be answered by a simple 'yes' or 'no.' You won't get very far.... Get your interviewee going by asking questions like:
    a. Can you describe...
    b. How did you find...
    c. Tell me more about...
    d. How did you meet...
    e. Where did you meet...
    f. How did you feel when...
    g. What do you see in this photo...
    h. What do you see in this album...

2. Start your questions with:
    a. How...
    b. What...
    c. Why...
        Rather than
    d. When or
    e. Who
        Since the last two lend themselves to short answers that may not help you much

3. Don't be afraid to rephrase a question if your interviewee seems not to be forthcoming, or confused about what you're asking. Just ask the same question in different words.

4. Try VERY hard not to interrupt an answer. You never know what you might hear that you didn't expect, or you might miss a salient fact or episode that your interviewee might have told you. If you cause someone to lose their train of thought you may miss something really valuable.

5. Ask follow up questions whenever you're not sure you understood what your person was saying, or you need more context for an anecdote, or you're not sure the person is telling you the truth.

6. You would be wise to write your questions down before your interview, and even some follow up questions just in case. I heard Dianne Rheem ask someone recently on her radio program, "Can you say some more about that? I'm not sure I'm understanding what you just said." Good question. Use it if you need it.

7. Don't let your ego get in your way. Don't be lured by an anecdote into telling one similar that you've had and then going on and on about yourself.

8. Please, please, please, don't lose your cool. Even if you violently disagree with your person, be polite. Bite your tongue. Being rude might very well cause your interviewee to shut down completely. You'll get through it.

9. Ask for specific examples of events or situations being recounted. You never know what you'll learn, and you want to have some 'color' in your narrative.

10. 'Bird walks' are absolutely OK. Sometimes. Don't worry if your interview gets off track occasionally. If the interviewee has fascinating side tales to tell you might really want to include them in your narrative. But don't hesitate to guide your person back on track when you feel the anecdote is running out of steam or has really gone around the bend.

11. Do encourage your interviewee, especially if he or she is nervous to begin with. You can use phrases like:
    a. Well said
    b. Well put
    c. That's helpful/that's very helpful
    d. How interesting!
    e. That's very interesting
    f. How in the world did you
    g. Where in the world did you
    h. You have a wonderful memory
    i. How did you ever

12. If you don't understand something your person has said, you might make a note of it and re-ask the question, or ask for clarification. There's nothing wrong with saying, "I'm sorry, I didn't understand what you meant by....

13. Reflect what your person is saying occasionally. You do want him/her to know that you're really listening. Reflective phrases are things like:
    a. What you said was...
    b. I think I heard you say...
    c. It's so interesting that you...
    d. I understand that...
    e. You seem to be...

14. You can end an interview with a variation of a technique I learned to ask at the end of a teaching session with adults. My questions always, always was: What do you know now that you didn't know before? You might ask: Is there anything I didn't ask you that you think I should have?

15. Record your interview if you possibly can with a small tape recorder, or now there are phone apps for recording. That's absolutely the best way of not leaving out some extremely important detail or anecdote from your manuscript. Just be sure you let your person know you're recording him/her.

Memoir Workspace 14: Pets

1. List every pet you've ever had. List them by name and then what type they were (if a dog or cat, for example). What made each one special to you? Add bullets if you've had a lot of pets.

-

-

-

-

-

-

2. What have you learned about yourself from your pet choices?

Memoir Workspace 15: Fame

What would you do if you were someone famous? As in: Steven King. Oprah Winfrey. President Obama. Cam Newton. Tiger Woods. Peyton Manning. Who would you like to trade places with? Why? And what would you do differently from what they generally do?

Serious Alternative Research:

If you had a peripatetic childhood, your parent was in the military and you moved around a lot; your parent worked for a company that transferred your family several times while you were growing up; you had a difficult childhood for whatever reason and you moved frequently from place to place, you might be missing some important pieces of your past. They may have disappeared from move to move. Or you may have a parent you never knew. So there may be chunks of information about your past that you really don't have, or don't have access to. If that's the case there are some other places you might not have thought of to find information for your memoir:

- Old cemetery records or headstones
- Old church records
- Bible records
- Birth certificates
- Death certificates
- Old deeds – to land or for businesses or for other types of property
- Marriage licenses
- Divorce papers
- Hospital bills
- Immigration or naturalization forms
- Wills from grandparents or parents or other people important in your past
- Draft cards and/or military records
- Cancelled checks
- Adoption records
- School report cards or records or testing reports
- Health insurance or life insurance forms
- Old newspapers – often archived on the newspaper's website (and, yes, most newspapers do have websites)

Public records like these are usually easy to get and especially simple to find on the internet. You can look up your state's archives on the Internet to find records. You can also frequently find all kinds of records listed on the web site of the county where you were born, or one of your parents was born.

You can go to the county where you were born and ask to see birth and death records and deeds. If you can travel, you might find some interesting information about your past that you hadn't even counted on or knew existed when you actually visit the county. Sometimes retracing the movements and steps of your predecessors can open your eyes to your own history. If you go, take photos; you never know when and how you might use them. I remember a huge old oak tree in my grandmother's back yard that we had a swinging tire on. When I revisited her house not long ago I felt the yard looked absolutely naked – the tree was gone! It didn't make any difference that the yard was neatly grassed and mowed. It just didn't look right! And it brought back memories for me that I hadn't thought about in a long time.

You can look on military web sites to find information.

You can find more than you ever want to know on Ancestry.com.

Banks keep records for a number of years, as do hospitals.

You can find interesting information on funeral home records. Or health insurance records. Or life insurance forms.

Don't think that just because you are missing chunks of information about your past that you can never recreate your life in the past. It may take a little digging, a little research, a little elbow grease, and maybe some creative thinking, but you can find more information than you might imagine by going back in time and looking through old records like these.

The most important thing to remember is that it's your interpretation of what you learn that is key, so you will get mileage of some kind out of lots of what you learn.

So don't get discouraged by a surface lack of information. Go digging….

Memoir Workspace 16: Five Things

Think about this:
What are the five most important things that have ever happened to you? Be specific and fill in what details you can remember. Like: what was it? Where? When? Who else was there, if anyone? What happened?

1.

2.

3.

4.

5.

Do you see any connections between or among any of these life events? If so, what are they? Note: these events may help you structure your memoir once you get to the writing part. If you find lots of connections, you might have a theme going and you can structure your memoir around a theme, like "My Life in Eight Moves" or "My Life in the Theater." If you don't see much for connections, you might want to structure your memoir on a straight time line (nothing wrong with that!).

Memoir Workspace 17: Decades

Think about each of the last five decades of your life. You young folks can think about the last two or three......What are the most significant things that happened to you or around you in each one of those decades? Label each decade (1980, 1990, etc.) Fill in what you can remember.

Important don't's – in general:

Careful there….. There are some things you need to be very careful about as you write your memories. And those things are mostly 'don'ts'.

Don't mush up (good technical term!) two separate memories if you can help it. Keep memories separate from one another as much as possible. There's a good reason for that: you don't want to confuse your readers, even if your readers are just your family. Sometimes two or three memories combined into one will lead you astray and turn out to be not the truth, which someone will invariably catch you out on. So don't try to get too creative and say, for example, that two incidents happened on the same day when they really happened a month apart. It's more important to remember them separately and let them stand on their own merits if they are important enough to include in your memoir.

Don't mush up any two or three people as you write. A temptation might be to try to 'protect' someone by not revealing to readers who the real person is, and so to fictionalize the person by mixing up his characteristics with another person, or other people. Don't do that! You don't ever have to use real names in a memoir, unlike in an autobiography. Remember that a memoir is your memories of people and places and things, not necessarily a heavily researched autobiography which should only tell facts and not emotions of other people. So just outline who the person is and don't give a real name. That's your privilege. Besides which, they really know who they are anyway…..

Don't change the chronology of events in your life. That means hard dates or events. If you're writing a thematic memoir you may skip around in time to keep the focus on your chosen theme, but don't change dates and times and places, especially dates. If you switch dates around to suit your sense of drama you may terminally confuse your readers, or even force them to think you're not telling the whole truth, which is a turn-off to readers. If you're not sure of absolute dates one thing you can do is put an event in the context of the historical time of that event. So, for example, if an event happened during the World Series of 1989. Or sometime right around 9/11. Or during Hurricane Katrina. Or around your college graduation. Or your wedding day. Close enough….. Just be sure you're telling the truth about times and dates as close as you can remember it.

Don't exaggerate any of the events in your life. You may really have suffered one or more traumatic events that you feel the need to write about. So write about those and the horrible circumstances that surrounded them. But don't at the same time overinflate some minor events in your life. That will only reduce the impact of your feelings about the true traumas. So, for example, if your car was rear-ended at a stop sign one time in your life, even though it was important enough for you to write about it, don't make that event out to be a totaling of your car and multiple cars and multiple injuries and hospitalizations and on and on and on. Anyone who knows you knows about minor events anyway, and knows they weren't that big.

Don't 'invent' conversations between and among your acquaintances if you weren't there. Don't quote people if you really weren't there to hear the actual conversation. That'll get you! Recreate what you can remember of conversations if they are that important to you, but don't put words spoken by other people in quotes if you can't verify that those specific words were spoken out loud. And don't ever - in the interest of creating drama – make up a conversation that never happened.

Don't describe in your own memoir what other people were thinking or feeling as they interacted with you. You can't possibly know what anyone else was thinking unless they told you face to face, or wrote their thoughts down on paper and sent them to you. Making up other people's thoughts and emotions is called *fiction.* That's not what you want in a memoir. You're not a mind reader (most likely). So unless someone tells you how they feel or felt or think or thought you need to step carefully here.

What you *can* do is intuit how people feel or think based on your knowledge of the person and their circumstances. If you know them really well you can probably get close to what they were feeling, but you need to be sure to state in your writing that you're making your best guess. People you've included in your memoir who are still alive will call you out for sure if you start attributing emotions and thoughts to them that they never had. So write about their thoughts and emotions as you interpreted them from their faces or their actions and maybe their words, but be sure you tell readers that you are interpreting what you see and feel, not what *they* think and feel. Your story is so much more powerful if you stick to what you can see and hear of other people. Your *own* thoughts and emotions are what we are really interested in, after all.

Memoir Workspace 18: Speed Memories

Set a timer for 6 minutes. Write as many memories as fast as you can off the top of your head. Don't worry about spelling or punctuation. The idea is to just go with whatever thought first comes into your head. Hang onto this sheet because you will probably end up with several events that you can plug into your memoir.

I remember..........

Memoir Workspace 19: Obituary

Write your own obituary.

What significant accomplishments would you like to be remembered for? What significant events? Keep it to 300 words, the usual length for a newspaper obituary. This may be uncomfortable at first but it really focuses your mind on what you have already accomplished and what you would like to accomplish before you die.

Managing your "plot"

The truth, the whole truth….. Managing, managing, managing.

In your memoir you don't have to feel obligated to tell everything you ever did, saw, ate, everyone you ever met, every place you've ever been. You do need to be truthful as far as you remember, but you don't have to stick to the truth only; you can go *beyond* the truth.

What does that mean?

That means that you can use a number of the writing techniques that novelists use, even though you're not writing fiction. And how do you do that?

First, you want to tell your readers a story. You want to create a narrative of your life that will flow from one incident or event to the next one. You need to let the incidences you write about build on themselves to a kind of crescendo – just like a music crescendo – and then hit reads with what the 'moral' of the stories is. Just like a good mystery writer would do, actually.

You want to manage, in writing, the pace of your narrative. That means that you want to keep a steady 'pace' with the narrative. Don't jump around or don't get so involved in describing one incident or one person that you run the picture into the ground. Keep moving smoothly from incident to incident or person to person. An uneven pace means you've got six pages on one topic and a line and a half on another, and your readers will *no*t like that. You want to manage the timing, in writing, of the events in your life.

In your memoir, especially if you're writing a thematic or episodic memoir, you need to manage the atmosphere of your mini-stories. Use a good selection of adjectives and adverbs to describe what's going on around you at the time. What's the weather? What's the time of day? What's the season? Is there a family gathering? A party? A funeral? A college campus? Your office? Your classroom? So, don't just talk about what happened to you, also describe the circumstances around you. The 'historical' significance of your surroundings may really be important to your narrative, so don't leave out those details. Please note colors and shapes and sounds and smells. Any good writer knows he wants to paint a picture for his readers, so the reader feels right there with him and you can't do that without great description. A memoir in straight black and white won't get your readers very far.

You also need to manage the tone of your memoir.

Is your memoir meant to be deadly serious? Funny? Light-hearted? Sad? Are you writing a morality play? In other words, are you writing a 'don't make the same mistakes I've made' story? Think about the incidences in your life that you are writing about. If you have had a number of sadnesses in your past life, and you want to get them out there, you need the tone of your writing to reflect that. That doesn't mean that you omit humorous or funny stories along the way, but you do need to write serious if you're writing about serious things.

Alternatively, if you're writing your memoir about all the wonderful things that have happened to you along the way, or you're writing about the love of your life (hmmm... loves of your life?) you want to keep your prose lighter. You want your readers to understand why you love this person or this place or this job or this..... You don't want to turn them off with turgid prose. You want to keep them with you.

Think about the book Julie and Julia, 365 Days, 524 Recipes, 1 Tiny Apartment Kitchen. In which Julie writes out her successes and failures at trying to recreate the classic recipes of Julia Child, and in doing so also tells the story of her relationship with her husband and those around her. So the story is Julie's but it also speaks to various relationships that we all have all around us. It's tone is sometimes serious, when Julie is having a bad day, and sometimes whimsical, on a good day, and sometimes really sparkling, when some recipe has turned out wonderfully!

Memoir Workspace 20: Interview

This is a *60 Minutes* interview. Think of at least five other people who will figure prominently in your memoir. Interview each one of them so you can draw them – in writing – very fully. You will discover along the way that you will need to make at least some other people in your memoir very fleshed out, so your readers will come to understand why each one is important to your life story – either positively or negatively.

Ask each person :

Person 1's name_____

Person 1's relationship to you: _____

- What's the best thing that ever happened to you? What did you learn from it?

- What's the worst thing that ever happened to you? What did you learn from it?

- Describe your ideal day.

- How would other people describe you when they first meet you?

- What do you like most about yourself? What do you like least?

- If you could have a different job from the one you always had, what would it be? Why?

- If you were in trouble who would you go to first? Why?

- What would you like to have written on your tombstone?

Keep going. You can copy this Workspace and use the same questions for Persons 2 through 5.

Now make some notes of your own about each person.

Personal information:

- Person's full name:

- Person's nickname:

- Personal history – family and backstory (where did this person come from and what were his relatives):

- Person's physical appearance:

    o Height
    o Weight
    o Age
    o Defining looks
    o Kinds of clothes he/she favors

- Person's personality, good and bad

- Person's schooling

- Person's talents, skills, gifts

- Person's mannerisms (sayings, habits, quirks, special personal objects)

- Person's main goal in life

- Person's secrets, at least as you know them (but proceed with caution here)

**What really works well here is if you make some "Character Cards" – literally. You can use old-fashioned 5 x 8 cards if you like pen on paper, or, if you are good on the computer, put your Character Cards in a Word document or on a web site like "Scrivener" which has 3 x 5 cards on line. Use one card for each person, or more if you need them. But keep your people's cards separate until you need to plug the individual person into your memoir. And, if you can, do these Character Cards before you even start writing. Then you'll have a picture of the whole person right when you need it.

What about the bad stuff?

What about the bad stuff that has happened to you? What do you do with that?

You don't have to write about any or all of those hurts. You need to give yourself permission to leave out anything that you find impossible to come to terms with.

But you might find that you really do need to include some of those bad/sad/hurtful/terrible/terrifying moments and events in your memoir, *if* they are important enough for you to remember them so clearly, perhaps after many years. And *if* they don't hurt someone else who was an innocent bystander. And *if* they don't cause extreme heartache for someone in your life who doesn't deserve it.

And *only if* you feel that recounting the incident or incidents will move your story line along in a constructive way. Most of the time confronting your own painful memories, or maybe painful memories you share with someone else, and writing them down will actually help someone you don't even know to understand how to deal with similar situations. So don't think you're just crying in your milk or just whining or just feeling sorry for yourself when you make the hard decision to write about painful stuff.

So what do you do if you feel you need to write about a death, a divorce, a terminal illness, a suicide, or some other really painful event that touched your life? It's a real danger zone, both for you and your readers, isn't it? Actually, your most traumatic life event may not have involved physical trauma, but you were spectacularly fired from a job and had the press at your door for three weeks. Your particular traumas are your very own and you need to own them even if you end up not writing about them.

As some memoirists have said, these memories may be 'emotionally radioactive material' to you, and perhaps to others. But remember that no one else has the same memories and no one else can relive those memories as you do. You keep yourself safe and your readers safe by recounting your memory of your trauma as specifically and truthfully as you can. And remember that you don't have to include every gruesome or excruciating detail if it doesn't suit your purpose.

The most important thing is to remember that that event is a memory, not your present life. You did, indeed, survive your catastrophic event. You've outlived the terror, the horror, the poison, the bad rap and come out the other side if not a better person at least a wiser one. In the present, remember that your job in life is to keep moving forward and not staying mired in the past. Just look at all the things you have accomplished! Look at all the things you still want to do! Look at all the chores you need to perform to keep yourself and other people moving on the road ahead.

One thing you might do is start out with writing down some 'field notes' about your particular trauma. Field notes are usually kept by people doing some kind of research out in the 'field.' The field may be literal or figurative but the notes serve as a reminder for the writer when he wants to sit down and put his research into a readable format. Anthropologists, for example, jot down random notes about old bones they find, just to remind themselves what they actually saw as they were digging. They may include rough diagrams of the positions of bones or the surrounding territory. But field notes also frequently include the writer's thoughts about what he found, the value or the significance of what he found. Field notes – written right in the field as the action takes place - serve the purpose of not letting the scientist forget anything that was important to his research when he gets back to the lab.

So you might say that your field notes are 'research' on your trauma. Even though your field notes could be being written many years after the fact, you're still doing a kind of research into your memory of the event.

Field notes at their simplest may look like:

What happened:	What I felt:
Details:	Reflections:
What took place to you and around you: the what actually happened and the who was involved Event 1: (what happened first and who was the instigator) Event 2: (what happened next) Event 3: (what happened next) Event 4:	What you were thinking as each event took place, as best you can remember. Or, given that your event may have occurred a long time ago, you may just want to write down your reflections at this moment.

Or:

What happened:	What I felt:
Diagram of the place:	Reflections:

If you are writing about one traumatic event, it might be easier for you to break it down to the pieces of the event as they happened. Or as you remember them happening. There's something powerful and liberating about confronting unpleasant memories and writing down what you remember. The 'Reflections' side is also a good place to vent your feelings about what took place at each point in the event. Get it all out!

Field notes are especially helpful if you had a very sad or tragic or upsetting childhood. The key here is to get your whole life events down, your most dramatic, traumatic memories out in the open on paper. Just write them down in chronological order (or a different order if you're not writing a chronological memoir). Don't cut anything out till you go back through your reflections. Remember: it's easier to cut out later than to try to fill in.

Or you may want to write a straightforward narrative on one or more paragraphs detailing what happened and then go back and add in your reflections. The field notes below were done in this format.

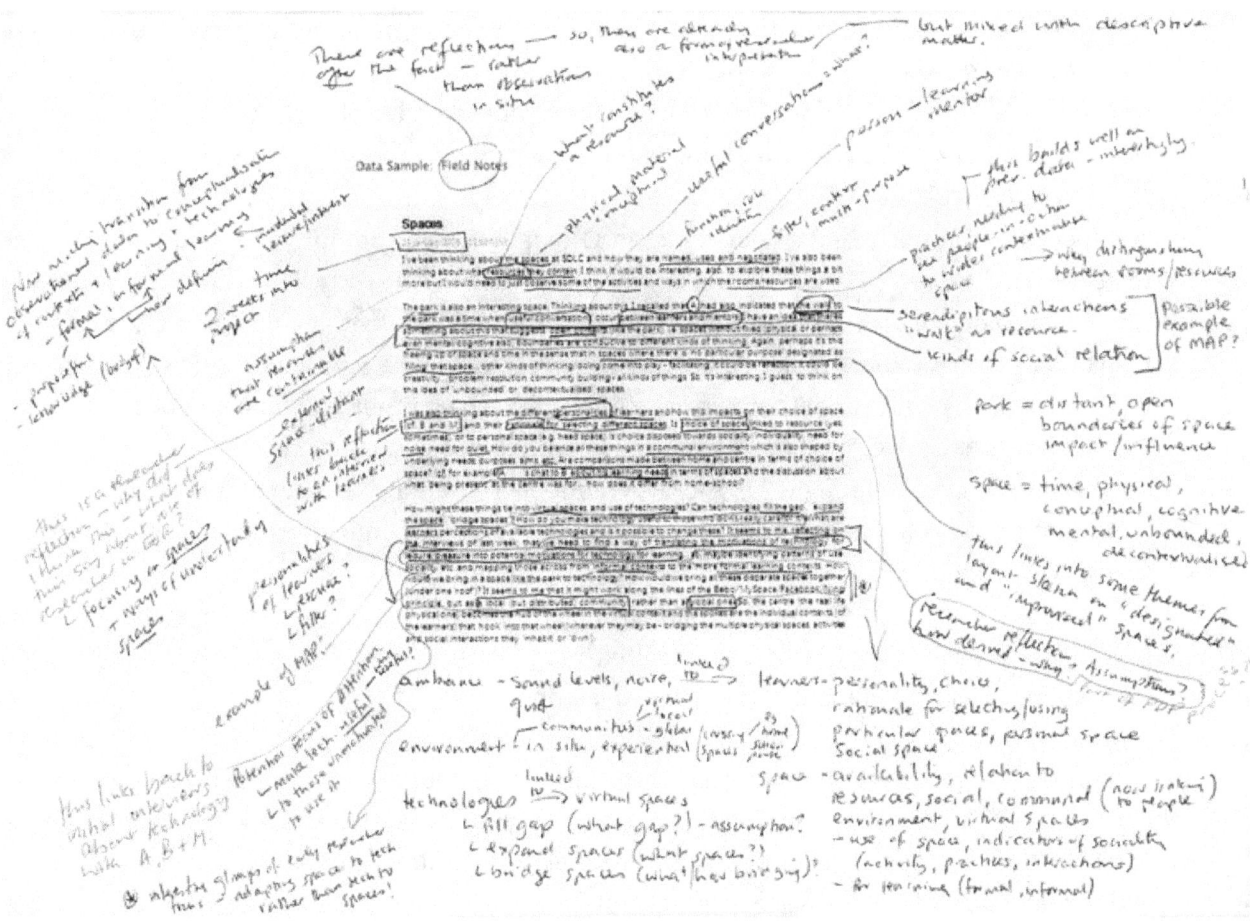

The important thing is to get something concrete down on paper, face the beast, stare it down, and then use your magic writer's wand to minimize it in your life. You may find out interesting things about yourself or others that you had never thought about before. And they may be really important to your memoir.

Something to remember: you don't necessarily have to recount your traumatic event all at one time in your memoir. It doesn't have to be one giant boo-hoo fest in the middle of your manuscript. You may pull out various bits and pieces as you go along, as they fit into your time line. You may want to divide up your details or your reflections as they occurred to you in your life.

If you've had several major traumas in your life, or your whole childhood was traumatic or upsetting to you, you really might want to space out the bad stuff and intersperse it with some good memories you have. After all, you did survive your worst nightmare! Your readers will appreciate the lessons you are teaching them: how to survive, how to thrive. How to forgive. How to find meaning in the evil things that have happened in your past. There's a reason, you know….. But your readers will also really appreciate knowing that you survived with a sense of your own dignity and worth, and that there is hope for them if they find themselves in a similar situation.

Some of the kinds of obstacles you might consider writing about if they have happened to you:

- The impact of a serious illness on you or someone related to you or perhaps your best friend or your best pet friend.
- How the addiction of someone close to you, or you yourself, has impacted your life.
- How you overcame an event that caused you great grief and what you learned from that experience.
- You feel you need to confess a deep dark secret that you have kept for years, and that you need to get out in the open.
- How you healed yourself –self-healing – from your traumatic event. Or how you came to some resolution about a major traumatic event in your past. Maybe your divorce was so painful to you that you really didn't deal with your emotions for a long time. Or you learned to live with a chronic illness and have come out better for learning to deal with it and move on.
- You had a major breakthrough – physically, emotionally, mentally – about something that is/was important to you and that perhaps confounded you for a while until you finally figured it out.
- You survived and came to terms with some kind of major crisis. Perhaps your spouse survived 9/11 in the World Trade Center – or perhaps not. The crisis you choose to write about may be of your own making – a business failure that taught you a valuable lesson – or a national or international crisis that taught you a valuable lesson.

And, finally, as you get farther into your memoir, you worry about *not* having any traumatic event to help you dramatize your life. But … it may occur to you somewhere along the way that your mother's death from a long hard battle with cancer actually influenced your choice of a career and therefore your whole life. Or that your dad's death in a car crash caused by a drunk teenage driver impacted your advocacy for programs to keep teens away from the alcohol and out of their cars if they do drink.

The main lesson here is that you don't want, as far as possible, to keep secrets from your readers. Get down as deep as you can with your troubled memories. Get as close to the truth as you comfortably can. If you only remember parts of your event, if the trauma was so severe that you've blocked parts of it, just tell your readers you're recounting what you remember, and they can take away what they will from your memory.

You may find that you free yourself from your past by writing down the yucky stuff and getting it out of your system. If you have ever felt terrible guilt or shame about something in your past, you may very well find that you' 66ve given it up when you get it down in writing. You may find that you have created connections with other people that were just waiting to be made.

In any case, it's out there now and you're done with it! Forever!

A classic 'memoir' of the *really* bad stuff, and I don't think there is any worse stuff, is *Night* by Elie Weisel. It is the often studied, most wrenching, story of his life during the Holocaust. It's heavy reading but ends up being so uplifting you will be glad you read it.

Memoir Workspace 21: Movie Rights

OK, you've finished your memoir and it's been published to rave reviews and it's on the Best Sellers Lists and it's selling like hotcakes.

And to top it off, you've just sold the movies rights to Stephen Spielberg for a huge sum of money!

- Who do you want to play you in the movie? Why?

- Which actors do you want to play the three other main characters in your life?

  o

  o

  o

- For a 90 minute movie, you can only focus on so many scenes. Which three scenes from your life would you want absolutely included in the movie?

  o

  o

  o

- So, is this an Oscar-worthy movie? Why?

Memoir Workspace 22: Conflict

Here's one that's different, but this kind of information might come in handy for you at some point. At the very least it might help you come to some greater, deeper understanding of yourself and how and why you are where you are today.

What's the angriest you've ever been with someone? Who is someone who has caused you pain in the past (or present, even)? Who is the person in your past or present who is most often in your face? If you could say all the angry things you wanted to say to this person, what would you say?
Write out your conversation. Feel free to say all the things you would never say in real life! Even if you are being hateful! Nobody's going to see this so go for it!

- What caused the conflict in the first place?

- When did this conflict occur – begin?

- Who is this conflict with?

- What has been the outcome of this conflict so far in your life?

OK, you go first. Start the conversation:

Him/her:

You:

Him:

You:

Him:

You:

Him:

You:

Him:

You:

- Has this conflict ever been resolved? Either positively or negatively?

- So how do you feel now? Better?

Section 2: Special Kinds of Memoirs

Thematic Memoir: the travel memoir

If you're a traveler, there are all kinds of possibilities for a travel memoir. In these days of memoirs that just cover part of a person's life, maybe your choice is to write about your travels: where you've been, what you've seen, who you've met. Sometimes a travel memoir can be as self-liberating and interesting as a memoir that catalogues your day-to-day existence. Your own curiosity about life in far (or near, for that matter) places you've found fascinating can lead to a wonderful narrative that will not only challenge you but reward your readers with a picture of life in other parts of the world.

You may just have a travel bug: you travel for the sake of seeing new places, getting away from home, getting out from under heavy business pressures. You never expected to learn any life lessons from your travels, you just like to go! You just love the places you've visited over and over. You love them so much you've decided to share your love and your lessons with others. You've discovered that a change of scene can create a whole new perspective in your thinking about other people and places, one that carries through to your better understanding of yourself and those around you.

There are several different formats for travel writing that you might tap into if you're a frequent traveler:

- The basics of getting from here to there and back again: the nuts and bolts; you've learned some hard lessons. Perhaps you've had a wild experience in the actual act of traveling, and you'd love to share the hard lessons learned and help other people avoid what happened to you. So you've got tips and techniques for packing, for running the airport gauntlet, for negotiating bus schedules in the Near East, for managing menus and food in Thailand. So you've got some really good practical information that's worth sharing to make other people's travelling easier and safer.

- You've fallen in love with one specific place, or one specific people and you've learned many interesting lessons about this specific place. You'd like to encourage other people to visit and to get to know the people here. So you'd like to write in great detail about one place, its colors, its local colors (the local characters), its history, its buildings, its peculiarities, its most famous crops or most famous business.

- You've fallen in love with the cuisine of one or two places, and you have learned how to cook or bake or grill the location's specialties. And you have created some really good recipes that duplicate or approximate the 'secret recipes' of your favorite place. And it makes sense to you to share what you've learned. Just remember, this is not a cookbook; it's a travel journal with a few - or several – great recipes thrown in. So remember that, although you're in love with your food, you need to focus as much on how the food fits into the place's history and culture. So your primary purpose here is to show the interconnectedness of the food to the place and the history.

- The long sad history of one place just fascinates you and you've learned some incredible historical facts that you think not many other people know. And you've done some intensive research that you want others to see.

- You've quite accidentally come across a very important archeological site in your travels, one that needs to be opened to the world. You've researched what the archeological finds mean in the grand scheme of things and you want to share your findings with the world.

- You love a change of scenery every now and then but you don't want to go far away from home. Luckily, there are some really wonderful kinds of secret places close to home that deserve a boost from your description of them.

- Or, you're a photographer at heart and you have some dynamite photos of the places you've been that are just begging to be made public along with the stories behind them. Just remember that this is a narrative with photos, not a photo album. Think about the term 'photo journal.'

So, how do you handle a travel memoir?

Well, first, as you travel keep a journal. That's the simplest way to recreate your memories. Write what you see. Take a few minutes either at bed time or first thing in the morning to record what buildings you've seen; what gardens; what castles; what cathedrals; what parks; what city squares. Or sit outside in a café in the middle of the day and jot some notes in your travel journal while you're waiting for lunch and smelling the wonderful aromas coming from inside the kitchen. Sit in a park close to your hotel. Sit in the garden of a chateau and people watch. You don't want journaling to become a chore, so maybe a glass of wine and a great view will give you the push you need. You want to enjoy your note taking.

Second, if you're not much into straight journaling, you might just want to focus on the one thing about the place or people around you that is most *different* from what you're used to. Describe the clothing of the Moroccan women you see. Describe the ancient buildings you see in Greece and make some note of why they speak to you. Describe the coming of age ceremony you see in Kenya. Describe the safari you're taking. Describe the funicular ride you have to take to the top of the Alp. You may be surprised what you learn about yourself from your descriptions of others.

If you feel comfortable doing so, talk to someone you meet in a faraway place. Talking to the local folks can sometimes open doors you never even thought about. At the very least you can learn how the local residents feel about their home, their town, their local politics, their local schools, national and international politics, and who knows what else?

Third, keep track of your photographs. Make note of what the photo is: what's the name of the building, the park, the chateau, the cathedral. Note the time of day and the weather. Who's in the photo? What else is in the photo? What's the dish you're enjoying? What's the name of the restaurant? Write the information down as soon as you can so you don't forget it. That is so much easier to do today with smart phones and tablets and Kindles. You can pretty much enter that information on a daily basis, if not an immediate basis. No excuses for not remembering when you get home what your photos are.

If you're an adrenaline junkie, describe your adventure while you're in it! Or as soon afterward as possible. Are you parasailing in the Caribbean? Are you bungee jumping off a bridge over a river in Tibet? Are you searching for old shipwrecks off the coast of the Carolinas? Are you climbing Mount Everest? What have you seen from high up? Who have you seen? What do you smell? What do you hear? What's it like to be you during your adventure? What particular insights and lessons can you pass along to those of us who haven't ever been where you are and probably will never get there physically?

You've just survived your mid-life crisis, in the middle of which you decided to get out of town! Get away from all the drivel and confusion and bad nerves and physical ailments. You've gone to somewhere exotic to get over yourself. In this case you might want to spend some time writing about what you learn about yourself in your travels. Think about the field notes we've covered. Make some field notes on your trip. Do the details of the places and people and sites, but then also do the reflections. How do you feel about what you're seeing, the people you're meeting, the history you're learning? On the other hand, how does it feel to let it all go and sit all day on a Caribbean beach? What have you learned from that? Think about all the colors of blue in the Caribbean waters. All the colors in the sands. All the kinds of trees. The peace, the solitude. What can you now let go of? What can you now consolidate in your mind? What lessons have you learned that you can pass along to others going through the same kind of crisis?

When you are in someplace besides your hometown, even if you're in a foreign country, there are resources you can easily find that will help you 'translate' your experiences for the rest of us. Don't forget libraries and all the print and video and audio resources they have. Check out the local newspapers for what's going on locally that interests you. Most international newspapers have English language editions so reading about your locale shouldn't be much of a problem. Also, check out magazines. Most international magazines have English language editions, too. You would be surprised at what you can learn about your locale from looking at what the locals are reading. Carry a little pair of scissors and a glue stick to cut and paste interesting articles or photos into your travel journal so you can refer to them later; that will surely help you jog your memory. And don't forget perhaps your greatest resource: the people you travel with and the people you meet on your journey.

When (not if) you meet interesting people in your travels you might want to jot down some of the attributes that made them interesting to you. What height was a person? How did he dress? What were his mannerisms that made you instantly like him? What were his patterns of speech that you found fascinating? What was so interesting that you remembered him when you didn't remember others? Adding some real people into your travel memoir can often help put your readers into the same location with you. Describing people you meet on the way adds life to the physical descriptions of the places you see. A travel narrative might be pretty dry if you only describe old buildings, no matter how beautiful they are. Put some people into your story to make the place interesting! You can add dialogue if you can remember it, or you can paraphrase the most interesting things you hear from someone you meet. It might be their patterns of speech that add the most to their description. At any rate, you need some real folks in your story to help you move it forward. Another good reason for carrying a little travel journal.

If you're a pretty decent photographer, intersperse some of the photos you've taken, ones that really speak to you, within your narrative. People who've never been where you've been generally love to see the photos; it helps to put context to the points you're making or to your descriptions. If you're good at sketching, include some diagrams of the places you've been. If you've been to Hampton Court Palace in England, for example, you might sketch a diagram of this huge palace, to help your readers see its beauty as you saw it. Sketch people you meet (if they allow). Sketch city streets, or cafes, or cathedrals, or famous bridges. There's a lot of life to be found in the sketches you make or your diagrams or your photos. They add color to your narrative in places where you might just need some color!

In the end, you will want to think about some major questions around which to focus your travel memoir:

- Who was I when I started out and how have I changed because of what I've learned?
- Would I have had this epiphany if I had never made this journey?
- How have I come to see my life differently now?
- What triggered this particular journey?
- What in my journey has inspired me most?
- What lasting lesson(s) will I take home with me?
- What have I learned that I can pass along to someone else?

A good memoir to check out for tone and on-target observations of strange places and sometimes strange people is *The Great Railway Bazaar* by Paul Theroux. It's a book that's been around for a long time and is now considered a classic. It is the story of Theroux's travels when he was young on trains across Asia, including The Orient Express. Theroux is among the classic travel memoirists, so any one of his book will probably delight you with their description, their wry humor and their detailed physical descriptions.

Memoir Workspace 23: First Birthday Party

When was the first birthday party you ever had that you can remember?

- Who was there?

- Where was it held?

- What were you wearing?

- What was your cake like?

- What was the best present you got that day?

- Did you play party games? If so, which ones?

So....how do you remember this birthday party overall?

Memoir Workspace 24: First Best Friend

Who was your first best friend?

- Where did you live?

- What was your favorite thing to do with your best friend?

- What about him/her drew you to this best friend in the first place?

- How did that friendship end, if it did?

- If you've lost touch along the way, how do/did you feel about losing touch with that best friend?

Thematic memoir: an illness story

You've survived a really tough situation. You might have had cancer. You might have had an organ transplant. You might be dealing with a mental illness. Or you've triumphed over an addiction. You might have survived a military conflict mentally intact but not physically intact. Or you might have survived a military conflict physically intact but not mentally intact. Or you might have survived mental or physical abuse as a child. Or spousal abuse. Or even something horrific like an attempt on your life.

And you have decided you have something to say about that.

An illness memoir is certainly a whole lot more serious than a travel memoir or the general story of your life. In the first place, it is severely focused on your specific situation. How you found out about your specific illness. How you dealt with it. What your behaviors were during your illness. How you reacted to treatment. How you reacted to major surgery. How you reacted to withdrawal. How you reacted to psychiatric counseling. How you came through the experience a better, or at least a changed, person. What you learned about yourself that you want to get off your chest. What you learned about others close to you that you want to explore or get off your chest. What you learned about the miracles of modern medicine – or not.

One way to tackle an illness memoir is to just tell your story in chronological order, as events happened to you. That may sound easy but it isn't always. If you'd like to follow this format, you'll need to go back and search your memory for lots of concretes: events; dates; specific people; specific places.

Then you'll need to set the scene for your readers: you're going to be telling a kind of 'before and after' story. So you need to lay some groundwork. What were you like before this misfortune? What was your life like? What were your physical characteristics and what were your behaviors? In other words, you need to describe your day-to-day life before. Who were you?

Then you need to move to the next phase: how did you find out about your illness? Who did you talk to? Who was (or were) your support? What was the diagnosis? Who made the diagnosis? What was the prognosis?

Third comes the actual description of your treatment. This is the hard part. This is where you need the names and dates and places. What actually happened, in order of when it happened. This will probably be the longest part of your narrative, since you most likely wouldn't be writing about a hangnail –over in a day.

Fourth: who did you meet along the way? Who impacted your life as you were going through treatment? Others with the same illness or the same situation? Others who have survived and have thoughts to share with you, for good or ill? What about your significant others? Your spouse, your parents, your children and/or grandchildren? Is there anyone who fell *off* your radar during your illness? Do you know what happened there? Which relationships survived and were they changed? The people stories of this type of memoir are important as much as the technical parts are, or maybe even more important. You do need to include any people conflicts you faced along the way, even if it still hurts to write about them. Those are every bit as enlightening and informative as anything you write about the needles and chemotherapy. They may turn out to be more important to some of your readers as they struggle through the same kind of situation.

The fifth part of a chronological illness memoir is your recovery. How did you recover? How did you know you were in recovery? Who told you that you were recovered? Who was with you? Who was your support group? How did you feel knowing you were over the worst?

The most difficult part of your story now is telling what you learned, or didn't learn. About yourself. About others. What is the moral of your story? What's the major point you want to get across to others? Where does this situation stand in the grand scheme of things? After all, you will have to relive one more time what you went through now that you have the words on paper. You will probably want to go back and read through your narrative several times to pick up on those important points that stand out to you now that didn't stand out while you were doing the writing. Pull out the two or three sentences that jump out at you as you reread. Those will end up being your 'aha' moments, the major points of what you learned as you wrote your whole narrative. Now spend some time writing your feelings and sensations about these critical moments. There you are: your story told!

However, suppose you're still dealing with pain and emotional turmoil and illness? What if you *haven't* recovered? What if you're *not going* to recover? Or you're not going to completely recover? Or what if you get better for a while and then regress. And then get better and then regress. Or your breast cancer is gone, but now the cancer has spread to your lymph nodes so you have to do it all over again. What if you've got a chronic illness that won't ever improve a whole lot: you've got sickle cell anemia or lupus or AIDS?

How do you handle that kind of plot line? Some memoirists call this a 'chaos narrative.' In this case your plot line is probably going to zig and zag around a lot, go forward and then turn around and go backward. Or sideways. Thus the 'chaos' term. This is your story if you've come to the realization that you're not going to recover. Or you've recovered to a point and you're not going to get any better so you have to learn to live with your condition forever, or for a long time.

You can still tell your story as it has happened to you. You probably still have things you think important to share with others, maybe so they won't lose their hope completely. Or maybe so they won't give up. Or maybe so they won't make the same mistakes you made along the way. But they *will* learn something from your story. Just follow the six steps above:

- Setting the scene
- The diagnosis
- Description of your treatment
- The people
- Your recovery – in this case how you found out you would not recover
- What did you learn?

Allow your narrative to wander around if you yourself did not progress in a straight line. Or if you found out that your treatment stopped here! And you're on your own. And you're at the end stage of your life or you're not getting any better – ever…. The most important part of this kind of illness narrative, and what's most worth sharing, is: what do you know now that you didn't know before? That's what your readers will want to know.

How does your situation connect with theirs? How do your feelings connect with theirs? How do your experiences connect with theirs? How does your pain reflect theirs? How do your fears reflect theirs? How does your uncertainty connect with theirs?

Finally: what wisdom can you share with others to help them?

Or:

What if you have a relatively common illness, serious or life-altering, but still one that everyone knows about, BUT you opt for unconventional treatments? In this case your story will more likely look like the chaos narrative than the straightforward treatment and recovery narrative.

Some of the differences you will need to take into account:

- What do your unconventional, less standardized treatments look like?
- What research did you do to point you in the direction of alternative treatment?
- What is the level of unpredictability of your treatments?
- Did you consult with any doctors or specialists at all? If so, why? If not, why not?
- How did the people around you react to your choices here?
- What kinds of conflicts did you face?
- How did you interpret the ups and downs of your treatment?
- How successful have these treatments been?
- What kind of prognosis do you have?
- In the final analysis, what lessons have you learned that are important to share?

Even if you have discovered that there is no longer any hope, think about putting thoughts and words to paper. Researchers find that many times a person who is going through a traumatic experience fares better during the treatment and frequently recovers faster and better if they write out their feelings along with their thoughts about their feelings. So even if you don't think about what you can share with others, think about that!

A memoir you might want to try is *Wasted: A Memoir of Anorexia and Bulimia* by Mary Hornbacher. It's the story of how she willingly got into drugs and sex and tried to starve herself to death, and then accepted that she was going to die, until one incident shocked her out of herself.

Thematic Memoir: passages in life

There are several prominent points in life of passage from one stage to another one. Years ago the writer and researcher Gail Sheehy wrote a book called Passages, which still remains relevant even today as we look at our own lives. The passages she wrote about were what she called:

- The coming of age twenties, when we leave home and start to set out on our own life journey as separate from your parents'. This is the point at which most of us find some kind of life partner (we think!) and begin to have our own children.
- The thirties, when we discover that we really need to hit the ground running. This is the make or break time for career and relationships, and all the hard stuff that goes along with solidifying both of those.
- The forties, when we begin to reassess where we are and where we want to go with the rest of our life. This is also the point at which we find the 'seven year itch,' both men and women. We lose a little confidence in all those youthful dreams and daydreams and begin to make sure we can put some reality into those.
- The fifties, when most of us have come to terms with all that youth stuff, and have solidified where we are and where we see ourselves heading for the rest of our life. In essence, we have resigned ourselves to what we are and we've decided to be happy with whatever that means and where we think we'll end up at the end of the road.

More recently Sheehy wrote a book called New Passages that challenges all of us to recalculate our life stages, now that advances in medical care are allowing us to live longer, healthier lives. So, maybe you're 45 now but you only feel 35; Sheehy says we need to drop back and recalibrate to the younger 'stage.' Think about that for a minute.

So there are several kinds of 'passages' memoirs that you could write.

The first is the *coming of age memoir.* Here you tell your readers about the end of your childhood and your journey into adulthood. To make the most of this type of memoir you focus on one or maybe two pivotal moments in your childhood that spurred or even caused this transition. Maybe you had an abusive parent and you want to write about the event that propelled you forward, out of that relationship. How you did it. What you did. What you learned along the way. What lessons can you pass along?

The coming of age memoir doesn't necessarily have to depend on a calendar age: what if your particular coming of age story occurred as you got free from an abusive spouse? Or you finally came to terms with your parents' life style. Or both your parents' deaths within a short time period. Or you came to terms with your adult child's addiction and the fact that you need to give up your overprotectiveness and enabling behavior. Or you had children when you were still basically a child. Or you found out as an adult that you were adopted and you want to tell the story of your search for your birth mother.

If this is the story you want to tell, search through your memory to find the one pivotal moment that you became an adult, your own personal 'aha' moment. What was it? Why did that particular event or place or situation impact you so powerfully? What legacy did it leave in your thoughts and feelings? Why is it important to you to tell this story? Start right there!

Once you have these thoughts noted and organized, tell your story straight through from beginning of event to end. That's the easy part. It's most likely chronological, so various sub plots should fall into place easily, even if some of them are hard to write about. You might follow the outline below:

- Set the scene: who were you *before*? What were you like? What was your life like?
- Who were the people in your life? What were they like? How did they behave? What did they do to you and for you?
- Who did you meet along the way that moves your story along? Who fell off your radar during your *before*? Or after? Why?
- What was your pivotal moment, your pivotal event? Describe thoroughly, even if it hurts. You may very well find that setting it down on paper liberates you from the emotional prison bars.
- What do you know now that you didn't know then?
- How do you feel now? Share what you feel, what you think.
- What lesson can someone take away from reading your narrative?
- What's the best part of your coming of age?

Another form of 'passages memoir' is the story of loss or tragedy. It's the story of one very painful experience you've had in your life, one that traumatized you in the past but you have outlived. Or it's the story of how you dealt with severe grief at one point in your life, perhaps the loss of a child or a spouse. Or a parent. Perhaps for many years you had a troubled relationship with your mother or your father, and your 'aha' moment led you to a renewed relationship. Or perhaps you had such a hard life for so many years that you tried to commit suicide more than once. Or – and don't sell yourself short here – the loss of a much-loved pet, that taught you many lessons.

This memoir is much more a relationship story than a treatment sequence or a fact after fact story of surviving an illness. So think about the people you want to write about, those who are crucial to your passage here, for good or ill. You will find that you spend more time in this narrative talking about your own personality and behaviors and the personalities and behaviors of those around you.

Different from a coming of age memoir, also, there may not be one pivotal moment that causes you to come out the end more successful than you went in. You may remember that you came to a gradual change through a series of small events, or revised, renewed, or ended relationships. You may have changed over a number of years, not in one sharp instant. So your notes before you write should include all those small memories of instances and people. Don't think that just because it was a small incident that it's not important. You're looking for a pattern in your own behaviors and in those of others in this passage story. Patterns are important here. What led you, maybe incrementally, to where you are so that you can tell your story?

The point to this kind of memoir is that you *did* live through it. You came out this end a wiser, if not better, person. So if this story is burning a hole in your brain you need to tell it. You may not realize what help your story may very likely give many others in a similar situation. You might follow the outline below, which is similar to the other passages outlines, but note the differences:

- Set the scene: who were you *before*? What were you like? What was your life like?
- Who were the people in your life? What were they like? How did they behave? What did they do to you and for you?
- Who did you meet along the way that moves your story along? Who fell off your radar during your *before*? Why?
- Has anyone fallen off your radar since your passage? If so, why?
- List the events that led to your passage from one stage of life to the 'now'. An easy way to do this is to go back to your memory notes (and your outline, right?) and just make a bulleted list of those things and people along the way that spring to mind. Then expand on the list to make your narrative.
- What do you know now that you didn't know then?
- How do you feel now? Share what you feel, what you think.
- What lesson can someone take away from reading your narrative?
- What's the best part of your loss/grief narrative? That may not sound right, but I'll wager you'll find some surprising bright spots in your memoires that are worth holding onto, and worth passing along.

You might want to try reading *Eat, Pray, Love: One Woman's Search for Everything Across Italy, India, and Indonesia* by Elizabeth Gilbert, the story of her 'coming of age' after a rancorous divorce, in which she travels to places she had never bee, by herself, and learns who she really is.

Or, try *Wild: From Lost to Found on the Pacific Coast Trail* by Cheryl Strayed, in which she recounts her hiking journey along the Pacific Coast Trail, by herself, in an effort to come to terms with her drug use, and her mother, and herself, and comes out a better person.

Memoir Workspace 25: Grandparents

Do you remember any of your grandparents?   Did you have an especially close grandparent?

If so:

- Describe a perfect day with your grandmother or grandfather. What did you do that you loved to do with them?

Thematic Memoir: the relationship (romance) memoir

You have a most unusual love story to tell. Or maybe you have just a plain old love story to tell. There's a reason that romance novels are always best sellers: everyone loves a good old-fashioned love story. Even if it's a new-fashioned weird love story. If it's a love story, everyone wants to know what happened and how it turns out.

You might have come to your love story later in life and that's what makes it so memorable to you. Or you met your partner in the most unusual of circumstances, or the worst of circumstances. Or perhaps your love story is long ago and far away. You may have just lost your partner of 50 years to cancer or a heart attack or a car crash. Or you just want your children and grandchildren to know where they come from.

Whatever your romance relationship is or was you want to memorialize it as the most important part of your life.

How is a relationship/romance memoir a little different from the other types of memoirs? Actually, in organization this memoir has more of a 'plot' than the other kinds. You might say that it reads more like a romance novel than a straight non-fiction narrative. Look at the outline below and then think of the romance novels you've read. In a novel:

1. First, boy meets girl. Girl meets boy. Girl meets girl. Boy meets boy.
2. The fire is kindled!
3. Uh,oh, there's trouble! (What kind of trouble? See below for some possibilities)
4. Boy loses girl.
5. Boy has to search in his own self for what caused the conflict.
6. Problem is solved (eventually, after a number of false starts)!
7. Boy finally gets girl for good.

Think about all the fiction you've ever read. You will realize that 99% of novels feature some kind of romance, even if they don't focus on the romance itself. And there is very rarely a romance novel hero or heroine that doesn't face at least one complication before the romance is consummated. And sometimes there are several obstacles to the romance that at first look seem insurmountable but the hero or heroine eventually finds a way around. So that's what your relationship memoir needs to look like. If that's what happened to you, you're in great shape for telling a compelling story!

Now, types of complications found in novels that could translate to your relationship memoir:

- The eternal triangle: your love is already taken by someone else. So what do you do to get rid of him or her?
- The 'Beauty and the Beast' theme: either you or your potential partner is scarred somehow. It could be emotionally, say, from a hardscrabble childhood, or physically, form losing a limb to cancer. How do you work around that?
- The classic Cinderella story: you, poor child in your rags, get the prince! How did you do that?

- The Hatfields and McCoys theme: your family and his/her family are mortal enemies and have been for generations. How do you get around that?
- The redemption theme: you meet someone in desperate need of saving, maybe from a terrible situation (is he a drug addict? Is she in an abusive relationship? Or in some kind of cult?) or maybe from himself or herself. How do you save him? Or how did she save you?
- The opposites attract theme: you are the quiet, shy one, or the one who doesn't talk much, who prefers to stay in the background, 'Miss Mousy,' and a cavalier shows up on your doorstep. He's brash and loud, cheerful and open to everything. Your exact opposite and you can't stand the sight of him at first. But you can't help yourself…. So what happens now?
- The stuck on a desert island theme: you and your seatmate, whom you've chatted with through your flight but have no particular interest in, survive a horrific plane crash and you're stuck alone in terrible terrain. You're faced with forced intimacy and physical dangers, which you confront together and which bring you together romantically. How did you survive and thrive here?
- The mistaken identity theme: you suddenly find out that your romantic interest isn't at all who you thought he was! Well, who is he really and how do you get around this sticky mess?
- The illicit love theme: you and your romantic interest have absolutely no business being together because… OOPS! What's up here?
- The forbidden love class/religion/race differences theme: you suddenly find yourself in love with someone everyone else thinks is absolutely not allowed!

So those are the main types of complications that you will find in a romance novel. And I'll bet you've got at least one of those in your own memories of your relationship and how it began. Write them out as you tell your history.

My husband and I are the classic 'opposites attract' theme. I'm the quiet, unshowy one and he's the outgoing, showy one (he checks himself in mirrors wherever he finds them). My colleagues gave us 6 months at the most when we were married. My mother (yes, my own very mother) tried to talk *him* out of marrying me because we are so different, and 42 years later here we are, our very own typical relationship story.

Your narrative here is pretty straightforward. Just tell it as it happened. You do have a lot of latitude here in recalling your feelings and your partner's feelings. Don't forget those; that's what makes your story so interesting.

Just one more note before you start your relationship memoir. All romantic relationships don't end in marriage. They don't all end in 'happily ever after.' That might be your relationship story. You might have been left for the other woman, or your partner just up and disappeared one day, or you went into the relationship knowing that it had no future but you were willing to accept it for the wonderful, temporary thing it was. If that's your story, and the relationship changed you in some mysterious way, go for it! You have lessons you learned that will apply to other people who will learn from your telling.

Follow a similar outline to the ones above:

- Set the scene: who were you *before*? What were you like? What was your life like?
- Who were the people in your life? What were they like? How did they behave? What did they do to you and for you?
- Who did you meet who became the most important person in your relationship?
- What kind of conflict(s) did the two of you face that put your relationship in jeopardy? Describe, describe, describe!
- How did you overcome your conflict?
- So who are you now?
- Who are the people in your life now? What are they like? Who *didn't* make it into your life now? Why not?
- What lesson(s) have you learned that has changed your life, made your life better?
- If your relationship didn't turn out so rosy, what lesson have you learned that you hope to pass along to people so they don't make the mistake you made?

A good memoir on the 'forbidden love' theme is *Kissing Outside the Lines: A True Story of Love and Race and Happily Ever After* by Diane Farr, in which she, a white woman, recounts her falling in love with a Korean-American and their struggles with gaining acceptance even in this modern world.

Memoir Workspace 26: Historical Life Changer

We all have occasions that are historical life changers. For example, if you're old enough, you remember exactly where you were and what you were doing when John F. Kennedy was assassinated. You remember where you were and what you were doing on 9/11.

Choose a world event that has happened in your lifetime.
- What was it and when did it occur?

- How did/has that event impacted your life in the long term?

- What meaning did that event have to you and to others in your circle?

Memoir Workspace 27: Gardens

Who in your life has or had a garden? Was it a flower garden or a vegetable garden, or maybe both?

- What did it feel like to be in that garden?

- Did you help in the garden? If so, what were your jobs?

- Describe the smells, the colors of the garden.

- How did that garden impact you long term?

Thematic Memoir: animal stories

Increasingly these days our family pets or other animals have become important to us, or even life savers for us. They do teach us lessons that other human beings can't get through to us, for whatever reason, our hard heads or theirs. Animals can sometimes serve as metaphors for major life events for us human beings. Or they can sometimes illustrate the ways we human beings *ought* to handle difficult situations just because they respond to harrowing situations with such calm and cool.....

Writing about your pet can be transformative for you. A beloved dog, or cat, or hamster, or snake, or whatever our animal choice, can sometimes tell us as much about ourselves as our best (human) friend can. By just writing about how you interact with your pet every day, you can gain some serious insight into your own personality, your worries, your sources of happiness. Memoirs including or wholly about dogs are especially popular. Think about <u>Marley and Me</u> by John Grogan, a memoir of supposedly the world's worst, most neurotic dog, who ends up teaching a family about what really matters in life. But if you've got a different kind of animal that has improved or changed your life, start there.

One thing you can do right now if you've ever wanted to write a book but didn't know where to start is to write about your favorite pet and what it taught you!

Even if you've never kept a journal, start keeping a journal of your daily life and interactions with your pet. Or maybe just some notes every time you have a funny or warm or totally surprising incident. You will be surprised at how well journaling works in this instance. For example, I note how my dog, Benji, a Shih Tzu, thinks he rules his little kingdom of our house. We actually frequently refer to him as 'Himself,' as you might a member of a royal family. When we take walks around the neighborhood, if we don't see any people often enough we have to stop where we are to look around for admirers. He's thinking, "Where are my peeps! I know I have many admirers in this neighborhood; why aren't they out here admiring me!" Now that he's getting older we sometimes refer to him as "The Curmudgeon." He's got the same crankiness that older people sometimes get: "No, I don't *want* to go that way, IT'S TOO LONG, I want to go *this* way this morning. And I'm going to stand here until you go the way I want to go!" These are the kinds of things you want to make a record of. These are your thoughts about your pet, but you can look through his eyes at how you react to him in various circumstances. You know your pet's personality after a very short while so just get your thoughts into some notes.

Make a list of your pet's 'characteristics' that are peculiar to him and no other animal.

- What color is he?
- What type of dog is he?
- How big?
- How much does he weigh?
- Who's his favorite person in the family?
- Who does he go to for comfort on a bad day?
- Who, if anyone, does he have 'arguments' with occasionally?
- What does he like to play with, if anything?

- Is he basically cheerful? Or not?
- Is he incredibly protective, of you or other members of your family?
- Is he laid back or nervous? Or maybe he has ADHD!
- How did he adopt you personally?
- Is he humble or proud?
- Does he like other animals?
- What's his most outstanding personality trait?
- What's the funniest thing he's ever done? The strangest?
- What do you like best about him?

If you've got, or have had, a pet that you feel taught you life lessons, don't be afraid to write about him.

Many times our pets teach us simple lessons, like slowing down a bit and enjoying the moment more. Or being more accepting of others we don't really care for all that much. Or accepting kinship with others; after all, we're all kin of some kind, even if it's from 1000 years ago. They sometimes teach us where we fit in to the grand scheme of things. They lead us to understanding of ourselves where we had little before. They teach us to enjoy surprises in life. To cope with disappointments with a degree of equanimity – as they do. They teach us what unconditional love looks like, a lesson we could all learn…. They teach us how to deal with death, too; it is sometimes as devastating when a pet dies as when a relative dies, if the truth be told. And they sometimes offer us the best life lessons we'll ever learn as human beings.

If you decide to write about your pet, or maybe other animals you've met in your life travels, you want to paint a picture with words. This may be a memoir without a sequential 'plot.' Here description is the key. There's probably no way you can over-describe your pet and his quirks and your reactions to him as life moves along. You might have a beginning, if you got him as a baby, and there might be an ending, if he has gone on to doggie heaven. But in this case it's the middle of the 'story' that we're most interested in. What's he like and what are you like when you're around him?

If you've got photos, or you're an artist, animal memoirs are a great place to include action photos or funny photos or sweet photos, or drawings if you're so inclined. Intersperse them with the text to make for a lively and colorful story line.

If you've got children, ask them for their feelings and their memories and the lessons they think they've learned from the pet. Include their stories in your text. You might even want to scan into your text the original notes or stories from your children in their own handwriting. Including their own tales can add depth to your story and make the words on the page that much more interesting to your readers.

Alternatively, write your memoir from your pet's point of view! Make him the story teller. What has he learned about you from his own perspective? What have you learned about you from his perspective? You might end up with a fascinating 'biography' of yourself and uncover things you didn't even know about yourself! Again, lessons learned….

Memoir Workspace 28: Prayer

Do you have a special prayer that you say often?

- If so, jot it down.

- When you say this prayer, how does it make you feel?

- Have you ever prayed for something specific? If so, what? Did it ever come to be?

Memoir Workspace 29: Siblings

Pick the brother or sister who influenced you most as a child. Or if you were an only child, pick a cousin or an aunt or uncle.

- Who was this person?

- How did they influence you? Positively? Negatively?

- Describe an incident that would show how this person influenced you.

- How do you feel now as compared with how you felt then?

Thematic Memoir: the spiritual journey

Many memoirists liken writing a memoir to taking a spiritual journey, to making a pilgrimage: both back through time and forward towards a goal that has nothing to do with the concrete realities of life. In writing a memoir you go back through a number of spiritual stages you might not have realized until you sat down to put words on paper. You may find that you have to let go of hurtful memories, of preconceived notions, of beliefs you've held for many years. You may find yourself writing of making uncomfortable discoveries about what happened in your past life, or your parents' lives, or your grandparents' lives. You find things you need to come to terms with before you die. How do you make sense of those things?

You might have come far away in your life from your original religious beliefs or training and you have set out on a new religious/spiritual quest. Or after many years you have returned to the fold, as it were. Or you have discovered a whole new spiritual path that suits you better than any path you have followed before. You're a lapsed Catholic. Why? You're a secular Jew. Why? You're a Southern Baptist but you've embraced the Kabbalah. Why? You have given up on organized religion totally. Why?

Is there a spiritual or religious moment or event at some point in your life that galvanized you to make a serious change? Or a moment that signified the permanent belief you have to this day? That might be a good place to start, if you're feeling the need to get your spiritual journey recorded, even if just for yourself. Finding yourself on this journey is the whole purpose for setting words to paper. This memoir is the story of your search for some kind of Divine Presence.

But: *big* but…. You may have had a spiritual 'aha' moment, but unless you actually do something with it you haven't got the makings of a spiritual memoir. What did you do *after* your spiritual awakening? Remember that a spiritual memoir is the story of a search for a deeper understanding of what has happened to you, what has awakened you or caused you to question or caused you to see life with new eyes. It's not just a compilation of your Sunday school lessons or your sermons or stories about your congregation; that's a part of a passages memoir perhaps or just a part of your general memoir.

Spiritual memoirs are hard work. You have to go way deep inside and look out. And then you have to write about the search. You may have to look back many years to tell the full story of your spiritual journey. And that may prove much more difficult than you ever thought. You might have to wade through years of alcoholism or drug dependence or losing your family because of your addictions. You may have to revisit a tragic accident or terminal illness of someone near to you. Or a huge fall from grace with the people around you. Things you hoped never to have to even look at again, much less examine minutely. But if these are the kinds of things that led to your spiritual awakening then they need to be accounted for.

Along the way you may have run into one or more – probably more – moral dilemmas that you faced with greater or lesser success. Did you become addicted to something or someone physical or emotional? Did you fail to help someone out of a sticky situation because you were too afraid or too comfortable where you were at the time? Did you not report child abuse of your spouse to the authorities? Did you lie on your resume? Did you actually commit a crime? These are moral dilemmas, for sure. What dilemmas you faced and how you overcame them successfully could be a major focus of your spiritual memoir. Your true character is revealed by how you have handled life's difficulties. How you have made ethical decisions, how you managed to do the right thing through adversity. No matter how little your past moral dilemmas may seem (now, we're not talking about not walking the dog two nights in a row because you just didn't feel like it) they add to your story of how you came to be where you are today. Here is the drama that will propel your readers through your story, and, remember, a good story needs a plot with some drama. So you've got that built in, in spades! *Your major story is what did you do with what you learned about yourself?*

However, you may find spiritual experiences don't come with a big bang. They come in the most common of situations or people or objects. So maybe your spiritual path has been through recognizing the Divine in walking the dog around the neighborhood. Knitting preemie baby caps for the local hospital. Teaching a class at a local Senior Center. Doing Meals on Wheels. Making dinner once a week for elderly neighbors. What have you learned over time from these otherwise mundane activities?

Spiritual memoirs don't need to depend on any specific religion or sect or variety of faith. They appeal to people of many faiths and religious sects. They tell the story of a search that could apply to anyone regardless of their religious preference. They speak to people on a much more primal level. What can anyone in the world take away from your spiritual memoir? What can they learn if they are faced with the same kind of difficulties?

One caveat: spiritual memoirs are not for proselytizing. You're not trying to sell vacuum cleaners here. Your purpose is not to convert anyone to your personal beliefs. If you do try that, your readers will never finish your story and may miss out on something they really need to hear. Your purpose is to tell a story that is so interesting, involving and enlightening that people will want to reread it to get as much out of it as they can. You want to tell readers about your evolution from one point in your life to a better point and show how you got to that point, not to tell them they need to get to *your* point. They need to get to *their own* better point, and maybe you can offer advice along the way. Remember: your audience will likely be from many cultures and many religions and many different faiths, so keep that in the back of your mind always.

Second caveat: *nobody* wants to read what a 'holier than thou' person has to say, so if that's you, get over yourself! It's your search for the Divine that we're interested in, not how wonderfully devout you are now.

You can use the following outline to help you get started on your spiritual memoir:

- Set the scene: who were you *before*? What were you like? What was your life like?
- What questions about your spiritual wellbeing did you have that spurred you on?
- Who were the people in your life? What were they like? How did they behave? What did they do to you and for you?
- Who were your teachers along the way?

- Who did you meet along the way that moves your story along? Who fell off your radar during your *before*? Why?
- Was there a pivotal moment, a pivotal event that led to your spiritual enlightenment? Describe thoroughly, even if it hurts.
- What moral dilemmas did you face along the way? (you might want to make a bulleted list here and then check off each one as you come to it)
- What do you know now that you didn't know then?
- How do you feel now? Share what you feel, what you think.
- What lesson can someone take away from reading your narrative?
- What's the most important part of your spiritual awakening?

A book you might try here is *Girl Meets God: A Memoir* by Lauren F. Winner, in which Lauren, the child of a Jewish father and a lapsed Southern Baptist mother becomes an Orthodox Jew but then becomes more interested in Christianity and subsequently converts. The memoir is the story of a year or her Christian life as she tries to reconcile her two religious 'halves.'

Memoir Workspace 30: Someone You Never Knew

Who is a grandparent or great grandparent, or other relative, you've heard a lot about but never knew?

- Write a description of this person as if you really had known him. Why is he or she 'famous' in your family history? What have you learned about him from the family 'archives'? What was he really like as far as you can tell from the family genealogy?

- The hard part, maybe: why did you pick this particular relative to write about?

Memoir Workspace 31: Important People

Let's talk about some of the important people in your life. There have probably been a number of people who have had some kind of influence on you over the course of your life. But there are probably a few who have had a profound impact on you. In your memoir you need to make these people three dimensional so your readers will better understand your backstory.

Pick three to five people from your present or past and write down the following information.

- Name:

- Relationship to you:

- Physical characteristics – height, weight, build, hair color:

- Daily schedule:

- Temperament:

- Job/profession:

- Marriage(s)/divorce/lost loves:

- Strengths:

- Weaknesses:

- Favorite foods:

- Scars or handicaps (physical and/or emotional)

- Most obvious traits (how she laughs, does she have tattoos, does she snore):

- Belief in God:

- Best friend, past and present:

- Enemies (why are they enemies?):

- Addictions, if any:

- Parents:

- Greatest fear:

- Sense of humor:

- General philosophy of life:

- Quirks and eccentricities:

- Speech quirks:

- What's the one most important thing your readers should know about this person?

- What's a one-sentence description of this character?

- Biggest impact on you personally:

Thematic Memoir: the business memoir

Boy, are these memoirs popular these days! Just look at the number of shelves in bookstores devoted to business books. And I'm not talking about economics books. I'm talking about books written by CEOs, successful or otherwise, about the lessons they learned from a business or the expertise and experience they brought to a business. Or by consultants who have saved the day for a business. Or by corporate types who have been brought in to dismantle and then 're-mantle' a failing business. Or by bright entrepreneurs who have created a wildly successful business out of nothing.

Business memoirs are different from other types of memoirs in one very specific way: they are written to promote your own personal brand to the world. You know something that no one else knows that will help some business to succeed, improve, or keep from failing. And you want to get it out there to sell yourself to others who could use your services, your expertise.

A business memoir at the very least is a kind of expansion of your resume. What have you done that turns out to be wonderful for your business? What do you want your next employer to know that will get you hired? What are the skills you possess that others don't have? How are you going to save their business from going under? How can someone else trust you to save their business or to take it from local to national to international?

There are several types of business memoirs that sell well. If you've got the idea, you might think about trying one of these ideas.

1. The history of your business:
    *   What is the business?
    *   What's your background that made you successful in this business?
    *   Did you start this business or did you inherit it or did you come in to save the day? Depending on which one, your 'plot line' will need to follow one path or the other.
    *   What did you do with it that made it successful? This is the story, so you need to go step by step with the concrete actions you took that worked.
    *   What special skills do you possess that you utilized? What's your area of expertise?
    *   Who were the people involved in its success and how did you find them?
    *   Why you? And not someone else?
    *   What's the lesson you can offer someone else in a similar position?
    *   What have you learned about yourself? That will have an impact on others?

2. You have a new business model or a quite different business model from the ones usually found in your type of business. Or you have found that an existing business model from a different kind of business will shake up your business and improve it. For example, sometimes educators find books about straight business models useful in improving schools and school systems. This memoir is about change at the highest and the deepest levels. It could be considered a turn-around memoir. How did you improve the business by changing it, from the inside out, or maybe from the outside in? You might want to follow the outline below if this is your thing:

- What is the business?
- What's your philosophy about this business?
- What is/was your inspiration for this new business model?
- What is your approach to making a successful business?
- How is your approach different from anyone else's?
- What did you do that made a dramatic change in the business: what steps did you take? This is the heart of your story so it needs lots of detail and examination.
- What special skills do you possess that you utilized? What's your area of expertise?
- Who were the people involved in its success and how did you find them?
- Why you? And not someone else?
- What's the lesson you can offer someone else in a similar position?
- What have you learned about yourself? That will have an impact on others?

3. You have a dynamite philosophy that has stood you in good stead with more than one business and more than one category of business. You want to spell it out so others can take advantage of what you have learned. This type of memoir is frequently written by wildly successful business CEOs who have reached the end of their business life. They are retiring and want to leave a lasting legacy behind. They've taken one business as far as they think they can and they are moving on to 'save' another business. The key point here is that your wonderful philosophy must be transferrable: it must have shown results over time and over several different kinds of businesses. So, you might want to follow the outline below if this is where you are:

- What's your overarching philosophy that's so winning?
- How did you arrive at this philosophy?
- How can you prove to your readers that you're legitimate?
- What is/was your inspiration for reaching this new point in your philosophy?
- What is your approach to making a successful business?
- How is your philosophy different from anyone else's?
- What did you do that made a dramatic change in the business: what steps did you take? This is the heart of your story so it needs lots of detail and examination.
- What special skills do you possess that you utilized? What's your area of expertise?
- Who were the people involved in its success and how did you find them?
- Why you? And not someone else?
- What's the lesson you can offer someone else in a similar position?
- What have you learned about yourself? That will have an impact on others?

4. And one of the most popular kinds of business memoirs is the rags to riches story. This is the story of your rise out of the ghetto, or from a devastated country, or from prison, perhaps. Or you come from a family that survived on mostly nothing, with many disadvantages. But you made your way outward and upward. And now you have a thriving business, a famous business, a multi-million

dollar business. How did you manage not just to survive, but to survive and thrive and come out the other end with a major successful business and life? You might want to follow the suggested outline below if this is your story:

- Set the scene: who were you *before*? What were you like? What was your life like?
- Who were the people in your life? What were they like? How did they behave? What did they do to you and for you?
- Who did you meet along the way that moves your story along? Who fell off your radar during your *before*? Why?
- What was your pivotal moment, your pivotal event? Describe thoroughly.
- What is the business you became involved with? In other words, how did you start out, where did you start out, what did you do to survive before you got your big 'break'?
- What's your philosophy about this business?
- What did you do that made a dramatic change in the business: what steps did you take? This is the heart of your story so it needs lots of detail and examination.
- What special skills do you possess that you utilized? What's your area of expertise?
- Who were the people involved in its success and how did you find them?
- Why you? And not someone else?
- What's the lesson you can offer someone else in a similar position?
- What have you learned about yourself? That will have an impact on others?

5. A sub category of the rags to riches story is the rags to riches with giving back at some point. If this has been your experience: you started from nothing, now you have much, and you decided along the way that you needed to contribute more than just your business savvy to your community or to the world. So tell your business story as you've lived it, but at some point add in where and when you first decided to give back. You might follow the suggested outline below if this is your story.

- Set the scene: who were you *before*? What were you like? What was your life like?
- Who were the people in your life? What were they like? How did they behave? What did they do to you and for you?
- Who did you meet along the way that moves your story along? Who fell off your radar during your *before*? Why?
- What is the business you became involved with? In other words, how did you start out, where did you start out, what did you do to survive before you got your big 'break'?
- What's your philosophy about this business?
- What did you do that made a dramatic change in the business: what steps did you take? This is the heart of your story so it needs lots of detail and examination.
- What special skills do you possess that you utilized? What's your area of expertise?
- Who were the people involved in its success and how did you find them?

- What was your pivotal moment, your pivotal event that caused you to decide to return something to the community? Describe thoroughly.
- What kind of giving back did you choose?
- How did you go about devising your plan for giving back?
- What steps did you take to set up your process: a foundation? A research center? A scholarship? What?
- What has your 'giving back' organization done so far that is worthwhile?
- Why you? And not someone else? What's your secret?
- What's the lesson you can offer someone else in a similar position?
- What have you learned about yourself? That will have an impact on others?

6. And last but not least: you could write a business memoir strictly for the purpose of getting rich and famous! Yep, that's true.

You are right in the middle of learning all kinds of business lessons that are making your rise in the world more likely and more successful. And you are on a roll. You don't have a multi-million dollar business to write about. You're not a world-famous CEO. You're still relatively new and young. *However….* You have a story to tell and lessons to pass along anyway. You can tell other young (and maybe not a few older) people how you are making such a success even while you're in the middle of the making. This is kind of a **self-help memoir.**

What are you doing right now that you feel could help others along the way? What's your purpose in writing this kind of business memoir? This is the key core of a rise to success memoir. It is really a kind of service story: a self-help book. But fortunately for you, this kind of self-help book will most likely not get lost on the shelf with all the other self-help books. This memoir will cause people to sit up and pay attention if they want to emulate your success: it's a business memoir, technically speaking.

Be aware that this memoir may be more difficult to write, since you're going through everything you're writing about *as you write about it.* You may find yourself writing at odd times of day or night. You might just be able to snatch a few minutes here and there. So don't go into this kind of memoir thinking, "I'm so wonderful and I'm moving right on up, and I can tell everyone else about my process and help them and myself at the same time." One caveat: for heaven's sake don't be writing your memoir on someone else's time! That will surely bite you eventually, and ruin your prospects and then you'll end up with nothing. This one is not a piece of cake. So don't approach it lightly even if you have great things to pass along to others, and you love to write.

If you're a journaler, here's a perfect place to put all your journaling notes together. Gather up all those bulleted lists of things to do and organize them so they make sense. All those office memos. All those 'lesson plans.' All those interoffice memos. All those phone call notes and e-mails and texts you've hoarded without really knowing why.

Go back to one of the outlines at the beginning of this book to get your notes in order. Start there. Then you could follow the outline below to help you get your thoughts even more organized.

- Set the scene: who were you *before*? What were you like? What was your life like?
- How did you get involved in this business?
- Who did you meet along the way that moves your story along? Who fell off your radar during your process or your *after*? Why?
- What event caused you to think you should set your process to paper?
- What is the business you became involved with? In other words, how did you start out, where did you start out, what did you do to survive before you got your big 'break'?
- What stage do you feel you're in at this point: very beginner? Somewhere in the middle of your rise? Finally near the top of the ladder?
- What mistakes have you made that others could profit from learning about?
- If you could have a 'do over' or maybe two – what would you like to do again so you could get it right this time?
- What's your philosophy about this business?
- What special skills do you possess that you have discovered? What's your area of expertise?
- Why you? And not someone else?
- What's the lesson you can offer someone else in a similar position?
- What have you learned about yourself? That will have an impact on others?

A memoir you might want to try is *Shark Tales: How I Turned a $1,000 into a Billion Dollar Business* by Barbara Corcoran and Bruce Littlefield, in which Barbara recounts her rise from a two-job failure to opening a very small real estate office and then to turning her investment into a huge business and much fame.

Memoir Workspace 32

When you were young did you believe in the 'one true love' theory? In other words, did you believe your prince or princess was really out there, just waiting for you? That there really *was* only one person who was the perfect match for you? The only one you could ever be married to?
If so, write about your 'younger' thoughts. If not, what was your child's view of love and marriage?

Memoir Workspace 33: Foodies

Interestingly, food plays a very large part in most families' lives. It's a rare family that doesn't have some food traditions or quirks.

Think about your own family.

1. I'll never forget one holiday meal with my family when...

2. My family's food traditions are...

3. As a cook, I often equate food with...

4. I am not a confident cook, but I can be counted on to love (kind of food) always....

5. My favorite food stories are........

6. Eating in my family is all about.....

7. When my family gets together for a meal we always end up talking about ....

Workspace 34: Meeting St. Peter

When you get to the pearly gates St. Peter has two questions for you before he will let you in:

1. What's the most important thing you ever did in your life? Why do you pick this one thing? No cheating – only ONE thing.

2. What's the one thing you left undone that you wish you had done? Why do you pick this one thing?

Workspace 35: Important Object

Have you had one object that has been really important to you in your life? An old doll? A blanket? A teddy bear? A favorite pen? A college poster?

What was it?

Why was it important to you for longer than most other things?

Do you know where it is now? Can you find it?

If you can find it – or even if you can't, just think about it – and write down what memories it stirs in you and why it was so important to you.

What does that object now tell you about yourself?

Harder task: can you sketch it?

Workspace 36: Sanctuary

What one space do you retreat to when you want some peace and quiet, or you want to calm your nerves, or you want to be left alone, or you want everyone else to quit bothering you just for a few minutes?

Describe. What place is it? What colors? Anything on the walls? What furniture, if any?

What feeling does this sacred space engender in you?

What does the space tell you about yourself?

Harder task: can you sketch it?

Workspace 37: What I Know

This is an adaptation of a teaching strategy teachers use when students tackle a new subject, but you can put it to good use even now. Think in broad terms about your beliefs now and what you still have to learn.

What beliefs and knowledge and skills are you proud or glad that you know at this stage of your life?

What kinds of things have you always wanted to know but you don't know, or know how to do yet, that you u still want to do or learn?

What I know now:

-
-
-
-
-
-

What I still want to know:

-
-
-
-
-
-

What can I do to learn what I still want to know?

-
-
-
-
-

What are some things I can tell people that will pass along what I know?

-
-
-
-
-

What are one or two concrete steps I can take to learn at least one of the things I still don't know? In other words, how am I going to go about learning something that's still in my 'bucket list'?

-
-

Now's the time so grab your courage…..
If not now, when?????

Workspace 38: When I'm Gone

What kinds of things do you want people to say about you after you're gone?

Thematic Memoir: the legacy memoir

This is the kind of memoir that you don't necessarily want to publish professionally. It may not be of particular interest to anyone but your family. But you want your children and your grandchildren and even your great grandchildren to know where your family came from, where it originated. And how the family got to where it is now.

Older people, especially, have stories to tell about their families that will be lost to future historians if they don't tell the story. For example, my father landed on Omaha Beach in the first wave on June 6, 1944. He tells me his story in bits and pieces. And sometimes I have to pry information out of him. But his story needs to be told. My mother's mother came on the boat from Ireland in 1909 and ended up being a kind of indentured servant until she was fortunate enough to marry. Her story – indentured servitude in this century – has not really been told, so I pick my mother's brain for what her mother told her about her early life.

Younger friends of mine have served in Iraq and Afghanistan and have incredible stories to tell. Their children won't know their stories unless they tell them. That might mean that the children will need to do some poking and prodding, but we need to know those stories.

I tell my older colleagues and friends all the time that if they don't tell their stories we will have lost an incredible narrative from our own history.

I tell my younger colleagues and friends all the time if they don't tell their stories we will have lost an incredible narrative from our own history.

My youngest sibling, a brother, died quite suddenly and unexpectedly at 47. I'm the oldest of five children, and the keeper of the family memories. It suddenly occurred to me that if I didn't start gathering up old slides, photos, programs, and other records, my brother's children might not have any idea of what he was like as a child, and might never know their important place in the family as a whole. So I did that for each of the remaining siblings, so their children will know who they are and where they bcome from and how they fit in.

So, all that being said, in particular, if you have an interesting or unusual family history, get it out there! Even if you just take your manuscript to the local copy store and print enough copies for the family, it's a gold mine for your family.

So, the major thing you want the younger members of your family to know is how your life was dramatically different from theirs:

- What was going on in the world? What was going on in your neighborhood?
- Did you 'survive' the Cold War? What *was* the Cold War?
- Were you a 60's follower of Ken Kesey? Who *was* Ken Kesey?
- Were you a Civil Rights marcher in Selma? Or did you have a close relative who can talk about the Civil Rights movement at its beginnings?

- Did your dad serve in Viet Nam? What are his memories?
- Did you follow the Watergate hearings day by day? What does the Nixon era tell us about history?
- Did your grandfather or great grandfather survive Auschwitz? What *was* Auschwitz?
- Did one of your relatives immigrate to the US from South Africa during the apartheid years? What *was* apartheid?

So you see where I'm going here. I am reminded of that famous saying about those who don't understand history are doomed to repeat it. Do we really want to relive some of those historical moments for good or ill?

Who were your other relatives and what part in history did they play, even if you just tell the story of your uncle Joey who paid his college tuition by being a soda jerk. Soda jerk? What in the world is a soda jerk?

So you might start by going back to some previous sections in this handbook and making notes from there:

- "Start with Mom and Pop", page45
- "Other Places to Find Information", page 40
- "Serious Alternative Research", page 51

If you do begin with "Start with Mom and Pop" here's how you can adapt the interview questions:

- How is the world different today from what it was when you were born?
- Who were the first immigrants to America in your family? When and why did they immigrate?
- What did the family enjoy doing together before you were born and when you were a baby?
- What's your first memory of your family?
- What's the funniest thing you ever did that you can remember?
- What's the strangest thing you ever did when you were little?
- What do you think is the most important decision you've ever made in your life?
- What's the most traumatic thing that ever happened to you? Or to a member of your family? Describe what you can remember, or what an older relative told you about that situation.
- What do you think is the biggest mistake you I ever made in your life? Why do you think this was your worst one?
- What's your proudest achievement in life (besides me, of course!)?
- What are the most valuable lessons about life have you ever learned?
- What's something, or several things, that happened to you or that you did when you were little, or younger, that you think I should include in my memoir? Why?

Just remember: do separate interviews, one with Mom and one with Pop. You might find quite different answers to the same questions. Keep the same question base but then add some questions that apply to your mom only and a few that apply to your dad only. For example, if your dad is a veteran you might want to ask him the most dangerous situation he ever found himself in as a soldier and follow up from there.

Don't forget to interview ex-spouses of parents and grandparents, aunts and uncles, siblings, half-siblings, step-siblings, if you can find them (and they'll agree to talk!). But don't despair: you can use a very similar set of questions to the ones you've used before:

- How is the world different today from what it was when you were born?
- Who were the first immigrants to America in your family? When and why did they immigrate? (for older relatives)
- What did the family enjoy doing together before I was born and when I was a baby?
- What's your first memory as a child?
- What's your first memory of your childhood (of me)?
- What's the funniest thing that ever happened in the family when you were little (or I was little)?
- What's the strangest thing that ever happened in the family (or when I was little)?
- What do you think is the most important decision you've (I've) ever made in your (my) life?
- What do you think is the biggest mistake you (I) ever made in your (my) life? Why do you think this was the worst one?
- What's something, or several things, that happened to you or that you did when you were little, or younger, that you think I should include in my memoir? Why?

Also, don't forget to look around your relatives' houses for such things as:

- Your folks' wedding pictures, or your grandparents or great grandparents
- Vacation photos are wonderful in this instance!
- Other photos
- Immigration papers
- School records
- Family Bibles
- And any other kinds of memorabilia they may have

Brothers and sisters? Ask them the same set of questions you've asked your parents. If you want to leave a family legacy they are important to your story. Even if there are riffs among some of them, or you don't speak to your sister but once a year, or your brother has had a substance abuse problem or you even lost track of your half-sister ten years ago, it's worth it to try and get their stories down to include in your memoir. After all, they are a part of your genealogy. And you might be able to get another family member to run interference for you: someone who *does* get along with the person you're worried about interviewing might really enjoy doing the interview for you.

A couple of caveats when it comes to close relatives:

- If you have a sibling or other relative who has had a traumatic event in their life, or has suffered greatly from some kind of addiction, or has some other secret known until now only by close family (or even known just to you) but you think that part of their life is important in your family's history, for heaven's sake talk to them first before you write about it for the world to see!

- Interview them to get their side of the story. You can do something as simple as asking them to relate their story chronologically from onset or occurrence to conclusion/solution – or not. You might want to use a small recording device if you have a poor memory, but let them know you're using one as an aid to your own memory, not theirs.

- Then let them read what you've written before going any further, and allow them to edit where they feel the need to.

- If you're faced with a hairy situation even after this, and their part of the story is of major importance to your memoir because their circumstance impacts everyone else in your family, you can always disguise them, as a last resort: change the name, change the city they live in, change their job description (if they have a job), change their mannerisms, but keep the story itself. Remember, you need to tell your best truth as you see it, so don't make things up as you go along.

- This is a 'don't even think about it!'- *don't* use your family memoir to get even with your brother whom you devoutly hate, your sister-in-law for whom you have absolutely no use, your step-mother, known to you as the wicked witch of the west, who 'stole' your father from your birth mother. You could be looking at a libel suit down the road if it comes out (and it always does these days…) that you wrote evil things about this person. Putting problems into the written word and then publishing that word, even if it's only your relatives who read it, can cause some serious issues. If you're lucky you're only going to end up having to issue an apology in writing. If you're not so lucky your wicked step-mother may sue you! In which case you may end up shelling out lots of dollars to said wicked step-mother. Now who's getting even?

All the caveats aside, you really do need to talk to all your closest relatives and get their memories organized if you are writing a family memoir. There should be enough of a story around you all that you can tell it with compassion, humor, understanding, knowledge, and truth.

On the good side. If you have them, space out your favorite family photographs through your text. Scan in some pictures of memorabilia that you think will add to the words of your family's story. Scan in birth certificates or marriage proposals or sports awards photos, or whatever you have in your memory box that adds to the impact or your family's story. You might in some circumstances want to show the not-so-pleasant side of your family's history, too. Did your grandmother survive a Nazi concentration camp and she has the tattoo to show? Put it in! Did your grandfather come over 'on the boat' and you have a photo of him on Ellis Island? Put it in! Was your uncle a rebel in a Middle Eastern country and you've got a photo? Put it in! You need to include those kinds of records too. In this day and time we are such a visual culture that any time you can include photos or photos of artifacts scattered through your text, you're going to attract more readers – even if they're just your second cousins.

At any rate, family memoirs may end up being the only actual record your descendants have of where they came from and how they got where they are today, and they are valuable to them if to no one in the public at large. So go for it!

A good Memoir you might want to try here is *Angela's Ashes: A Memoir* by Frank McCourt, in which he tells his story of growing up as he says in "a miserable Irish Catholic childhood." It's a dark story, hard to read in some places (my mother had a hard time getting through it since her mother was raised in similar circumstances) but the 'moral' of the story is that McCourt survived to do what he always wanted to do: write compelling stories.

Workspace 38: Life Left?

OK, you have been told by your physician that you have at most only one year left to live. What's the ONE thing you want to do before your time runs out?

Workspace 39: Family Heirloom

Do you, or does your family, have an heirloom? An object that has special significance? An object that has passed down from one generation to another? A ring? A tiara? A baseball? A soldier's medal? A quilt? If you do, describe it. What color is it? How big? What shape? Was it handmade or store bought or awarded? What mental pictures does it put into your mind? What sentiment? Who does it remind you of?

Harder task: can you sketch it?

Thematic memoir: the food memoir

The most important thing to note here is that this is *not* a cookbook! It's a memoir that includes stories about food and maybe some recipes along the way, but not a straight cookbook.

Food memoirs have become very popular in the last few years. Think about it: everybody has to eat. And everyone has some sort of particular culture that they grew up in and that culture often expressed itself in part through specific foods, or specific ways of dealing with food.

Food habits are also part of almost every individual family's own culture. How your family folds into a larger culture is of interest to other members of your extended family, if to no one else. Just think about Southern home cooking. Soul food. Sushi. Thai food. Comfort food. French cuisine.

Think about food rituals in your own family. Think about sitting around the family table at Thanksgiving. Sitting around the table on Fridays for the Sabbath. Sitting around the table at Christmas. Birthdays. Anniversaries. Graduations. Even family funerals.

Whatever your family's genealogy, you probably have food stories to tell.   Mama's candied sweet potatoes are a requirement at Thanksgiving. Aunt Margaret's oatmeal cookies are a requirement at Christmas. Dad's fudge is a requirement anytime, especially if you get to take a spoon to the warm leftovers in the fudge pot! My dad was the fudge maker in my family with a secret recipe that he refused to share with anyone – he even refused to allow anyone in the kitchen while he was making the fudge! And it only came to me after he had a stroke and couldn't make it anymore.

What you think about food and how you express yourself about the foods you know and love can tell a lot about what kind of person you are – think about that for a minute. What does that say to you? When you think about all the people sitting around the table at a holiday you don't just think about what's on the table; you often reflect on the characters of the people around the table, on their quirks and personality peculiarities and their jokes and their love lives and their children and their jobs, and, and, and....

Actually, you don't have to be an expert chef yourself in order to write a food memoir if you have a passion for food and you have wonderful stories to tell around certain foods or meals or recipes or other cooks, or just your family memories in general.

And don't feel that you have to include recipes for dishes. You might not have them. Or the story revolves around the people at the dinner table most importantly and the food, while important, is still secondary to what's going on around the table.

And the 'table' can be anywhere in the world. It doesn't have to be at your home or your mom's home. You may have fallen in love with Italy in part because you have such warm memories of Florence's outdoor cafes where you could spend an afternoon watching people go by over a good glass of wine and you discovered that Italian pizza is very different from American pizza. Or you scraped up enough money to spend five days in a classic French cooking class in Provence. Or you were introduced to callaloo in Jamaica and fell in love with it and the people. Or your grandmother survived a Nazi concentration camp and has old old old German Jewish recipes that she's passed down to you. Or there's a 'famous' borscht recipe that has migrated to this country by way of your great grandmother and only your family has the recipe (until now!).

So what you might be looking at is the story of your life through the lens of food, or foods. Or maybe the story of your life with a few food stories thrown in at appropriate points. If you have always had a close relationship with food, work your 'food tales' into your memoir.

Sometimes the food stories you have to tell are a metaphor for your whole life. Think about that! Think about Julie Powell's memoir Julie and Julia: 365 Days, 524 Recipes, 1 Tiny Apartment Kitchen. We learn as much about Julie and her striving for a life that made sense as we do about the recipes as she cooks her way through Julia Child's The Art of French Cooking.

Or think about your battle with cancer and chemotherapy and the fact that you couldn't taste anything after chemo sessions or you couldn't eat anything without getting sick so you learned what you could eat and learned to make it yourself. So you created recipes that really would work for many cancer patients. Get them down as part of your story!

One thing to remember though: food narratives need to tell a story the same as a general memoir does. If you don't have an overarching story to tell, food stories won't save your narrative. Even cookbook authors know that!

So, for the good of the cause: I love to make my Christmas gifts for my neighbors each year. They are what an old friend of mine always called 'love gifts' which show you love someone or appreciate them but the gifts aren't big enough to take a lot of money or a lot of time to make. The neighbors always appreciate them because we live in an old historic district that has recently grown a crop of hard working young mamas who don't have the time to do some of the neat little things they'd like to do.

Chili-Lime Ketchup

Stir into ½ cup of ketchup:

1 minced chipotle pepper

Juice of half a lime.

Herb Mustard

Stir into ½ cup of mustard:

2 tablespoons of chopped fresh parsley

1 teaspoon each of minced thyme and rosemary

<u>Pesto Mayonnaise</u>

Stir into ½ cup of mayonnaise:

2 tablespoons of prepared pesto

2 tablespoons of chopped fresh parsley

You can spoon each one of these little condiments into a little decorative jar (or even a small Ball jar), put a decorative cloth square around each top, tie with a neat bow and you've got wonderful love gifts to give out. Each one of these takes about five minutes to prepare and five minutes or so to wrap up, so you are good to go! These little condiment jars have stood me in good stead for lots of years. I just vary the herbs and spices and keep on giving. I know the neighbors appreciate them because they keep giving me back the empty jars to refill!

See how easy it is to include a recipe where it's appropriate in a narrative?

Workspace 40: Family Food Traditions

What is one of your family's most sacred food traditions? List the food(s) and make some notes about how the tradition arose and why it remains a tradition.

Workspace 41: Family Characteristics

In order to write a good memoir it helps if you describe family and friends very well. The people who surround you are sometimes very important in your story so it helps the reader if they have at least some understanding of your circle of family, friends, and acquaintances. Prepare a list of characters. The people who have had enough impact on your life that you are going to include them in your memoir. You can list them by name since this exercise is for your writing notes and not necessarily for publication; if you decide you need to you can give some persons a pseudonym after you get all their information down. Next to each name include any personality traits you can think of:

- Relationship to you
- Favorite foods
- Daily schedule
- Quirks and eccentricities
- Physical description (height, weight, coloring, build, eyes, hair, identifying physical marks like tattoos, etc.)
- Temperament
- Weaknesses
- Strengths
- Family connections
- Job/profession
- Add some characteristics of your own
-
-
-
-
-
-

Don't skip this exercise. This part is like writing a novel: we need to understand your characters very well in order to sympathize with them or hate them or believe in them. But enjoy the exercise; have fun with the characteristics of each of your people.

You can also cut these 'cards' apart when you get through with them and rearrange them into a new story line whenever you want to, sort of mix and match.

Person 1:
Name?
Description:

Person 2:
Name?
Description:

Person 3:
Name?
Description:

Person 4:
Name?
Description:

Person 5:
Name?
Description:

Person 6:
Name?
Description:

Person 7:
Name?
Description:

Person 8:
Name?
Description:

Person 9:
Name?
Description:

Person 10:
Name?
Description:

Workspace 42: Guest Reader – Style Editing

When you get to a kind of natural stopping point in your narrative give it to a good friend to read through, and ask him/her to answer the following questions about the manuscript. You might really want to do this exercise several times throughout your writing, not just at the end. A thorough reading of your manuscript by someone not too close to it could really help you move forward, and might keep you from going down the wrong path and then having to spend a lot of time rewriting.

Don't get all defensive about what your guest editor says. Wouldn't you rather have her point out problems before you submit your manuscript to a publisher, who turns it down because of too many interior problems with the writing?

Ask your friend to:

Read the manuscript through without marking on it. Then think about:
- How would I improve the manuscript? What things would you change? Add? Delete? Rearrange?

- Does the opening page make you want to read on? If yes, what makes it so effective?

- If it could be improved, what would you do?

- Does the manuscript writer use effective topic sentences for each paragraph? And does the topic sentence help develop the paragraph?

- Does the writer use sufficient details and examples? If so, tell where the writer has used detail effectively, quoting directly from the manuscript. If not, suggest where the writer could incorporate more details and examples.

- Are there any words, phrases or sentences that aren't clear? If so, offer the writer some suggestions.

- Do you see any problems with spelling, grammar, or punctuation? Don't fix their mistakes but indicate the problems they need to address.

- What's your overall impression of the narrative?

Thematic Memoirs: What else is out there?

Now, just in case you really want to write your memoir but you haven't yet found a format that you've absolutely fallen in love with, there are several other kinds of memoirs you could put together. Look at the list below of out of the ordinary structures for memoirs and see if one of them speaks to you:

- Your diary! If you're a diarist you might go back to your diary entries to find a thread through most, or many, of them that are worth putting together.
- Your life through music: your favorite songs. What memories, what events, do your favorite songs tell about your life?
- Your life through photographs, a photographic memoir. What do your photos say about your life? What about who's in them? Who's not in them? Where were they taken? What were the circumstances surrounding each one?
- Your life through letters. To you and from you.
- Your life through media: emails to you and from you, Facebook posts from you and to you, blog posts – yours or those you're referenced in
- Your life as a movie! If you are fortunate to have old videos, whether in black and white or color get them organized to tell your life story. Reputable camera shops will work with you to splice together old videos and mesh the black and white with the color. It doesn't make any difference if some of the snippets have dialogue and some don't; as long as they tell a cohesive story your viewers can fill in the blanks.
- Your life as a scrapbook. If you are a scrap booker you have enough craftiness or artiness to put together a scrapbook that can serve as your memoir. If you really love scrap booking you can make copies of photos and do separate scrapbooks for each of your children. And if you really really love scrap booking you could do a slightly different scrapbook of your memories for each child that focuses on that child.
- And you could actually do a cookbook, like a traditional cookbook but with stories to go along with the recipes.

Workspace 43: Fascinating Place

What's the most fascinating place you've ever been? Maybe a foreign place? Maybe somewhere in this country? What made it so fascinating? Talk about colors, sounds, smells, people, sites, anything that made you fall in love with it.

Workspace 44: The Do-over

If you could have one do-over for anything in your life that you've ever done, what would you want to do over?

Why?

What would you change?

Final Thoughts:

- You have a remarkable, one-of-a kind story to tell.
- If you don't tell your story no one else will! And think what we might lose if you don't tell your story.
- Setting your story to paper may very well lead you into a greater understanding of yourself even if you never show what you write to anyone else. And how could that be bad?
- Telling your story is a great legacy for your descendants.
- Celebrate each step along the way. Don't look at stumbling blocks as reasons to quit. Go off in a different direction – go where the stumbling blocks lead you. You never know what interesting things you might learn that you never knew you didn't know.
- You have your own style, your own preferences for writing. So go for whatever format you feel most comfortable writing. There's no 'correct' way to set up a memoir.
- You have your own personal body clock. If you really feel at your best writing from 1 to 3 AM, go for it! I know, I know, you have a real job from 8 to 6, but if you do your most creative thinking in the early AM, you will inevitably figure it out.
- Also, you might keep a notebook and pen right beside your bed if your insomnia gets you thinking about some really great stories you want to include in your memoir. Just jot down enough words that will make sure you remember what you were thinking about.
- And **the only hard part about writing a memoir is that it won't' write itself.** That's something you've got to do. And many times if you set yourself a specific 'writing space,' maybe from 9 to 10 PM, at the kitchen table, after you've put the kids to bed, you'll get into a comfortable habit in no time. Just don't guilt yourself into stopping the writing because you can't stick to a rigid writing schedule. It would be lovely if you could write for three or four hours at a time, but unless you're Steven King or Louise Penny or Paul Theroux, you probably don't have that luxury. So for heaven's sake write when you can where you can and then don't worry about it. As long as you're getting words onto paper, you're doing good work!
- And finally: everyone has a story, including you!

About the Author:

Kathy Tuten has basically been a teacher all her life. As the TV commercial says, it's what she does.....

Kathy is the author of nine handbooks on topics ranging from how to decide what to do with an aging, ailing parent to teens' guides to writing different kinds of novels (their first best sellers!) to how to help difficult children learn not to be so difficult to how to deal successfully to difficult colleagues in your office without losing your job. An eclectic mix of topics but when you're a teacher......

Kathy has been an educator for more than four decades. She was a teacher, a curriculum coordinator, an assistant principal, a principal, and a school system level instructional officer, all in her first professional life.

In her second professional life she taught at the University of North Carolina, where she was an assistant director in the nationally known and respected Principals Executive Program. In this program she taught principals, assistant principals, district office personnel and school boards the tenets of leadership: what makes an exceptional leader on the local and national level.

In her third professional life she worked for the State Education Superintendent of South Carolina in the capacity of the Director of the Office of School Leadership, again working with educators to encourage the practice of better leadership styles and methods.

Kathy has a B.A. in English Education from Pennsylvania State University, an M.Ed. in Education from the University of North Carolina, Curriculum Specialist Certification, Supervision Certification, and Advanced Administrative Supervision from the University of North Carolina, and has pursued post-graduate studies at the University of North Carolina.

If you have any questions, don't hesitate to contact Kathy at k.tuten@live.com .

www.ingramcontent.com/pod-product-compliance
Lightning Source LLC
Chambersburg PA
CBHW081216280526
45787CB00006B/2423